Winter's Love

A Tribute to How the Human Spirit Rises Above Expected Limitations

K. T. Oliver

Kay Taylor Oliver

ISBN: 978-0-692-03208-4

Library of Congress Control Number: 2016937201

Printed in the United States of America.

"What is love" was the most searched phrase on Google in 2012. Numerous psychologists, sociologists, religious leaders, and philosophers have debated the answer to this question since time began. Every culture has its own interpretations influencing poets, authors, playwrights, composers, and individuals all over the world.

GIVING THANKS

Words cannot express my profound appreciation for so many people who inspired me as I wrote *Winter's Love*. There are groups of people, such as my intimate circle of girlfriends and a special group of women whom I affectionately call "my girls" who continue to amaze me with their precious friendship. I share my most intimate secrets with "my girls" who inspired many of the vignettes in this book, and so I wish to recognize them for their special input. So to my sisters Karen Staten and Carol Clay, my girlfriends Wanda Herndon, Marjory Johnson, Eula Dean, and Sharon Elliott, thank you for loving and believing in me.

There would not be a book without the guidance, probing, and pushing of our personal Cupid, Joyce Daily-Buford, who I thank every day for introducing Walter to me. Then there is Mama 2, I am Mama 1, who adopted my dog Ginger and loves her as her own. I wish to also thank Patricia Crenshaw whom I recently met. Pat decided to read my manuscript backward to make certain it flowed with interest and to design the next steps in the rollout of *Winter's Love.* I selected four additional readers who all had a specific task: Laura Davis, my daughter, who read for sensitivity; Tiffany Staten, my stepdaughter, who read for clarity; Carol Clay, my sister, who read for spiritual correctness; and Joyce Daily-Buford, our dear friend, who read our story for accuracy since she followed every stage of our love's development.

In addition, an informal survey was given to fifty men asking them each to give ten qualities men find attractive in women. Twenty-three men of all ages, races, and marital status responded. I shared with them that I would not give their names unless they had no objections. I want to thank the following men for their input: Chuck Hughes, Bob Martin, Mike Sims, Terrance Staten, Eric Taylor, and Wallace Wortham. I also want to thank the remaining respondents who wish to remain anonymous for their input.

Finally, I thank my husband Walter Oliver for being my muse for this book. At times I knew it was embarrassing for him because he is so "low-key and under the radar," but his thoughts, actions, and certainly his love inspired me to write about the intense love that happened in the winter of our lives.

Kay Taylor Oliver

TABLE OF CONTENTS

What Is Love
By Walter Maurice Oliver

Love is defined by God. His love is unconditional and is a model of what true love is. There are no conditions, demands, or expectations required for God to love us. It is the love the prophets speak of when they convey God's desire for us to love one another as we love ourselves. God's love is continual, ever enduring, and always there, regardless of any of our human failings.

Looking back on my childhood, my parents gave me unconditional love. I may have disappointed them at times, but I never doubted their love for me; their love was never in question. I was loved completely regardless of my behavior. I was encouraged to choose my own path knowing that they supported the choices I made in my life. I watched them give that same unconditional love to my sons, never comparing them but praising them for their unique personalities. The love they modeled for me is embedded in my being and has allowed me to share that same unconditional love with my children, my wife, and others with whom I have a close relationship.

I believe loving unconditionally comes from God, and I believe the very nature of human beings' love is based on conditions. Conditions such as: if you believe a certain way, treat me a certain way, are like me, etc., then I can love you. This type of love will never allow you to experience the full meaning of a love based on your relationship with God.

Once you believe you are loved for yourself and for no other reason and that you love yourself based on God's love for you, only then can you love others unconditionally. Unconditional love frees you to accept and be responsive to others versus responding to your ego. Unconditional love gives you the foundation to be free to give wholeheartedly to others by giving all of your affection to someone else. You naturally express love by being caring, forgiving, kind, patient, hopeful, supportive, and selfless.

Unconditional love does not demand love in return or depend on certain beliefs; it simply acts with tolerance in every dimension.

Prologue

What do you mean they're getting married? Didn't they just meet? Didn't he just lose his wife? How many times is she going to marry? I heard that her father told her sister to keep doing it until you get it right. Geez, I haven't had one husband yet and here she is getting married again. Do you know who he is? He has a condo in Phoenix and only comes once or twice a year. And she met him? No, no, a mutual friend introduced them and now they are getting married. I want to know what she is doing to get these men.

So there it is, how did I get this man and why do I want to share my life in such a public forum? I want to let everyone know that no matter how young or old you are I know there are two things that are for sure. First, love knows no boundaries unless you create them. And second, you never give up on what you want out of life; you just ask and it will be given to you if you believe. So, this is a story about how two people who fell in love after giving up on finding real love again. Both had experienced love and marriage and felt they had been blessed with living their lives with people who were loving, good, kind, decent, and moral—quite a combination, a combination that rarely exists, but they were both fortunate to find. Both were content and felt God had blessed them so they simply decided to embrace their families and live their lives as best as they could without the partners they once shared everything with.

Although lonely, each found they could fill their days with lots of activities, events, organizations, work, family, and friends. However, if they were truthful, although content, they were still lonely but thankful that they experienced their partners as long as they did especially since so many people, even though married, appear lonely. Some are still married, some never married, and some just dated one person after another never finding the right emotional bond that two people feel when they fall in love. So, all in all, these two people were very lucky or as the one would say to the other, very blessed.

People say that when you want to write about something that has great meaning for you that you should write from the heart. That is, just start writing and let your thoughts flow through your fingers. Well, that is what I am attempting to do, write from the heart about the most significant thing that has happened to me in the winter of my life. I won't set a stage for you by giving the time or place, simply an accounting of what now seems to be the hand of God on the lives of two people who found love after experiencing great loss. Therefore, I write this book for those who have given into the shadows of doubt: *It's too late for me. I will never find someone to love me. Why am I looking for the perfect person who does not exist? I am going to settle for what is in my life now, in other words as Luther Vandross sang, "Love the one you're with."* Well, I write this book to say it is never too late for love, so open your eyes and look around. Better yet, look at yourself and see the beauty that God created in you, only you—the unique you. You are a gift that some wonderful person is waiting for.

Winter's Love

A Man or "The Man"

I feel accomplished! What a strong word but that is what I feel, accomplished. I have had an outstanding career with a bittersweet ending, holding positions that few women have held but yet not reaching the highest level in my career. However, all in all, by my own standards, I feel I have achieved what I set out to accomplish. Certainly we all want to reach just one more pinnacle, but in my mind, leaving my nine-to-five job to pursue whatever seemed important to me was truly liberating. After all these years, I could do things my way. In other words, I could finally do what I know in my heart is fundamentally just and right.

I am for all practical purposes a writer. I love it; I feel I was born to do it. When Rick Warren wrote *The Purpose Driven Life*, I immediately identified with him simply because I always felt purpose driven in everything I ever attempted to do. For whatever reason, I put my heart in my work and I got out of it exactly what I put into it. Joy.

I am happy and fulfilled, I have everything a person could want, a beautiful home in Scottsdale, Arizona; wonderful children and now grandchildren who are the essence of my being. How marvelous is this life? What more could I want? I am reminded of that question each time I attend an event and see other women with their husbands or significant others. I feel a little pang and then I meet up with my girlfriends, some married but most single, and we laugh and tease each other asking, have you met anyone yet? That conversation quickly grows into online dating. *Have you tried it?* Those who have share their experiences, the good, the bad, and the ugly, and you secretly say to yourself perhaps I might find someone.

There are phrases that we women use when dating men who just don't seem to be "THE ONE." We make up names to describe them to our girlfriends, such as No Shoulders, The Gump, Scary Man, Egg Head, The Negative One, etc., and what is so funny is that through the years we discuss these men as if the names we made up for them were their real names. Our conversation goes something like this, "The Gump called me the other day and I tried to tell him that I just was not interested without hurting his feelings." Or, "Is it me or am I so blinded by Egg Head's twisted idea of what he thinks is an intellectual conversation that I can't see his positive qualities?"

Following these conversations, we would begin our assessment of what we were really looking for in a man. The usual list is shared: single—meaning never married or not separated but divorced—tall, good looking, employed, living in his own place, able to speak in complete sentences, dresses well, clean and groomed, and has a passport. I threw the last one in because most of my girlfriends and I love to travel and we are tired of traveling with each other.

During these deep girl-talk conversations, we would analyze our list and try to think of what qualities we could eliminate, after all no one is perfect. Our rationale was if we found a man with most of the qualities perhaps we could help him develop the ones he was missing. But then we shout, we want all of them because this is what makes us happy.

So how do you find the one man with most of the qualities you are looking for? But wait, there really should be three questions. How do you find the man, how does the man find you, and how do you get the man to fall in love with you? First things first! Finding the man is really simple. He is out there. Finding him depends on your final and absolute list of must-haves. Does he have to be tall and good-looking? How about employed and living in his own place? Then there is speaks well, is well groomed, and has a passport. What if you could cut this list in half and still find the love of your life? The statistics of cutting your list in half just increased the probability that you would find a good man, a man you could respect and yes, the love of your life. After all, isn't respect more important than any of the other qualities?

Does he have to be tall? There are degrees of tallness. Do you mean at least taller than you or do you mean basketball player tall? What do you mean when you say *tall*; does height have anything to do with character? I don't think so. How about the passport? I know I threw it in but now I am throwing it out because if you fall in love with someone, you can always get a passport. But now, in steps reality and there are certain must-haves.

During my dating years, I had my fill of entrepreneurs. My girlfriends and I were death on any man who said he was an entrepreneur. In our minds they were always "entreing" and never "preneuring." So job is important to me. You can be self-employed or working for a company but making money to sustain yourself is important. Therefore, as long as you are employed you can have a roommate; sharing the rent/mortgage is cost effective and sometimes necessary in this economy. What about living with your parents? Depends on the conditions. Is it temporary? Are you there to help them or are you there for them to help you? Is this a short-term arrangement or has it been since high school? The latter is a red flag on how the person conducts his life—too dependent for me.

My next must-have is being able to speak in complete sentences, none of the following: "Are you feeling me?" or "Know what I'm saying?" I need complete sentences with words I can understand and draw conclusions from. And finally I need a man who is well-groomed. I also like and want a well-dressed man but I will take well-groomed over well-dressed any day. I don't want to enter into a person's life only to find out I need to ask him to shower daily!

So I cut my list in half but now I am adding something that never seems to be first on anyone's list: Morals! I need a man with morals. I can give up a lot when I see a man with morals. Not that I am a Goody Two-shoes, but I think I have basic characteristics that are built on a moral platform. Therefore, I need someone who can provide that same morality. I could continue to add attributes like a good sense of humor, thoughtful, on time, etc., but these are above and beyond the basic list that my girlfriends and I discuss so many times. So, I need a well-spoken working man who has his own place, is well-groomed and has morals. I can work with that.

Wait a minute! What about me, what do I have to offer? It's clear what I want in a man, but how do I attract the man

I want? Psychologically people see themselves, as they want others to perceive them. Are we a perfect 36-24-36? Are we attractive, well-groomed, and well-dressed? How about our personal life? Are we single, divorced, widowed, have children? Do we live with our parents or do we have our own place. Do we have a job and what kind of job do we have?

Right now, I am overweight. Despite knowing this to be true, I continue to think I am camouflaging it with my choice of clothes. What if the man I want does not want a woman with weight issues? We could go on and on: what if he doesn't want a woman with short hair or gray hair (a nonnegotiable for me), a woman with children, or a woman who doesn't have a job? All the "what-ifs" are only hypothetical on my part because I don't really know what his final and absolute list of must-haves is. Then how do you attract "the one" based on your list if you don't know his list? And therein lies the problem, how do you create a match? Can you control it or is it really out of your control and you submit to destiny, fate, or the will of God?

I can't speak for my girlfriends, but I have had some pretty bad experiences. For instance, I was standing in FedEx Kinko's waiting for a print order and this good-looking man approached me and started up a conversation. He fit all of our surface characteristics: tall, good-looking, speaks beautifully, and is nicely groomed and dressed. He asked for my telephone number and I gave it to him. Leaving Kinko's I was excited. He called, we arranged to meet, and, as a precaution, I told my girlfriend when and where so she could pass by to make certain everything was okay. We met in a little restaurant and had a great conversation that evolved into a lot of laughing and slight touches on the shoulder and hands. I was loving this! My girlfriend rode by as planned. But wait, I digress, what was she doing in that vintage expensive convertible with that old man? It turned out he was her online date who said he was much younger than he actually was. She said she couldn't cancel because she was supposed to make certain I was okay. But who would make certain she was okay?

My Kinko's friend was wonderful and everything was going so well. After a few glasses of wine he said, "You know you are so special and I really want to get to know you better, but I want to share something with you." I was smiling and thinking I want to get to know you better too. And then he said it", "I'm married." What! I was so taken aback that I just looked at him, got up, and went directly to my car. He was following me saying, "Wait a minute, you don't understand we are having some difficulties." Yeah, sure. Then he spun me around, like in a romantic novel, pressed his lips on mine as though he really thought he was so appealing that his kiss would change everything. I pulled away, jumped in my car, and drove off. He called several times, thank goodness for caller ID, and that was the end of that.

Okay, that was one bad experience. But I didn't give up. A good friend called to say that she had some friends coming in town for a doctor's convention and one of them wanted to have a date for the awards dinner. That should have been my first red flag. I mean, a single doctor needing a date? However, my girlfriend insisted that he is a great person and very well thought of in the medical circles. So she gave him my telephone number and we decided to meet for cocktails prior to the dinner. In walks this obnoxious loud talking guy in his late 100s already plowed with liquor and a mouth as foul as any gutter. I could not believe my girlfriend would set me up with this person. So, I thought just go to the dinner and then disappear. I barely made it through the dinner because I was so embarrassed. My friends saw me with this guy and were dumbfounded. Oh, did I share that I was in a turquoise gown from Paris? Needless to say, I quickly but quietly made my exit. Why would a girlfriend introduce me to such a loser? Perhaps because she thinks I am desperate. Do I look desperate?

Still need more examples? Okay how about being asked out to dinner only to find out after you are dressed to the nines, including Chanel bag in tow, that he, the date from hell, takes you to a fast-food restaurant? Now there is nothing wrong with fast-food restaurants except for on a first date. When a man says, "I would like to take you out for dinner," perhaps you are thinking, sit-down dining, menu, wine, etc., or is it just me? No, I am sure most women expect to go to someplace nice for a first date. It doesn't have to be expensive; a picnic in the park is not expensive but it is impressive.

It is not just me! Let me tell you about one of my girlfriends who is extremely intelligent, very beautiful, and makes tons of money. She decided to try online dating and one of the men who contacted her asked if he could take her out to dinner. She agreed to meet him at the restaurant he suggested. After meeting him face to face, they chatted but she was not really into him; there was just something strange about him. Then the check for dinner came, and sat and sat . . . and sat on the table. The date finally looked at my friend and asked if she would pick up the cost. She replied no, but that she would pay for her dinner. He seemed very uncomfortable and began searching for his wallet. Once found, he pulled out a bill folded so many times that it was folded to approximately a square inch. He slowly unfolded it as my friend looked on. She decided she could not take anymore and called for the waiter. She paid for her dinner and then left the restaurant as her date continued unfolding his single bill.

If you were to get your girlfriends together, you would have hundreds of stories similar to the ones I have just shared. But wait, to be fair, what kept us going is every once in a while we would hear of someone meeting a wonderful man and getting married. That happened to my sister. She went online and met a wonderful man. After talking on the telephone for almost a month, they finally met, fell in love, and married. So, we throw up our hands and turn to the Internet dating services to help us find our perfect match. We fill out our online profiles and complete several questionnaires and then . . . there it is, a list of characteristics we are looking for in the man of our dreams.

My girlfriends and I get together to laugh about the guys we have dated, but once the laughter subsides we discuss the need to have someone special in our lives. Some of my friends want to get married and some just want a relationship. As for me, I just wanted someone to go out with, someone to share the days' events with, someone to plan a vacation with. Marriage was out of the question. I had the love of my life, a great marriage that ended all too soon because of cancer. I have been loved, treated like a queen, and always made to feel special. I had someone who cared about how my day went and what he could do to make me happy. He would wake up in the morning and say, "Good morning sweetheart." Who says that? I'll tell you who, people who are really in love and really care, that's who.

So, back to the original question, how do you attract the man of your dreams? I went online to see what experts suggest you can do to make a man fall in love with you. What I gleaned after reading for hours is that everyone has their own perspective on the many facets of love, which leads me to believe that everyone has their own list of must-haves. The writers of these articles are speculating based on what they think and feel you are thinking and feeling. Their advice is presented in a broad range designed to include as many descriptive types of people as possible, thus allowing every person reading their rendition of love and attracting love an opportunity to see themselves as possible benefactors of their wisdom. My takeaway to most of the articles I read suggest that anyone can find love if they follow the advice outlined sometimes in stages or more often in convenient steps. This is like the majority of weight-loss programs. If you do all of the things proposed, you could lose weight. The people that I have seen lose weight are mostly on television pushing some form of a weight-loss program and they look like they are twenty-three. The rest of us in the real world did not continue with step nine and that's why we are overweight.

The final conclusion that I reached after all of my reading is simple. When I am in public—at a mall, theater, or restaurant—I sometimes look at couples and wonder to myself how in the world did she get him or how did he get her? My mind whirls to the only logical answer: love. He loves her and she loves him. It is clear and obvious. Their love has nothing to do with a final and absolute list of attributes. Each person threw away must-haves on their list to accommodate characteristics that the person of their affection possessed. Sometimes you hear a person say I fell in love with her because of her infectious smile, or he has a sense of humor, he is so attentive, she is caring. I have never heard anyone say when first asked why he or she fell in love with someone that it is because she is so beautiful or he has a good job. Oh, by the way, I am talking about real love.

So let's throw away our lists and start all over with the intent of finding real love. There is no list just some helpful advice that you can use or not use that may remind you to look at yourself through a different lens. Perhaps you can think of it this way, although Michael Jackson was speaking about the atrocities in our world and how we could be instrumental in solving them, he reminded us to look at the man in the mirror: "Take a look at yourself then make the change." This one line speaks volumes about so many aspects of our lives that begin with looking at ourselves first to determine what we can do to create change. Instead of making a list for what you want in a man, why don't you make a list of your attributes and then create a plan on how you can improve yourself for you! I want to make me better for me, and that will take a lot of work if I am honest.

I Have Someone I Want You to Meet!

It seems a lifetime ago when Joyce, a friend who belongs to the same women's organization that I do, asked if I would be interested in meeting someone whom she is very close to. I did not know it at the time but Joyce has introduced other people who have ended up in serious relationships including marriage. She has an intuitive gift that emerges when she sees two people who she feels would make a perfect couple. As I look back on our conversations, I discovered Joyce is very deliberate with her matchmaking. Unlike many well-intentioned friends, she studies each person looking for matching qualities instead of looking merely at one's single status. Why does she do this? She simply says it makes her happy and she likes to see others happy as well.

So I said I would love to meet her friend. Joyce's prior husband and his friend, Walter, attended the same college and after graduating, they continued to be good friends. Sadly, Joyce's husband died, but after some time she remarried. And then, Walter's wife died, and through it all, Joyce and Walter remained friends.

Every year our organization sponsors a golf tournament. If possible, Walter would attend as Joyce's guest. This particular year Joyce was very pleased that Walter graciously made a contribution in memory of his late wife. After one of our tournaments Walter and Joyce sat together and she pointed out all of the single ladies and asked him if he might like to meet one of them. He simply avoided the question or said something like he wasn't quite ready yet. She always ended their conversation with when he was ready she would like to introduce him to a friend.

On another occasion Joyce asked him how would he feel about meeting someone and he seemed indifferent. That did not deter Joyce. As a matter of fact, she took it as a yes and called me to ask the same thing. I said yes immediately because as I said earlier, even though I was very content with my life I liked dating because it gave me an opportunity to dress up and enjoy a man's company.

You have to know Joyce. She is very task oriented and once she decides to do something she stays with it until it gets done! Joyce planned a luncheon for Walter, who lives in Virginia but would be in town to take care of some business with a condominium he owns in Phoenix. The rationale for the luncheon was to thank him for the contribution he was making to our golf tournament. When she discussed the details of the meeting with Walter, she once again asked him if he was ready to meet someone. This time he asked about me, the very person Joyce had in mind for Walter to meet. Joyce was elated and called me to set up the luncheon on my calendar, sharing that as president of the organization I should attend. I agreed.

It was a lovely spring day and Joyce, her husband Jim, Walter, and I met for lunch at a restaurant in a shopping plaza across from his condominium. I took a quick peek at Walter and he was pleasant looking, very well-groomed and casually dressed in a silk shirt and dress slacks. He has great eyes, a shaved head, no facial hair, and stood about five feet, seven inches. I wore a sleeveless embroidered mesh top with a great short tan skirt that zipped up the back and helped to accentuate my legs and hips (you always dress to impress). I parted my hair on the side and let it fall into a soft curl just above my shoulders. As I was looking at him, I saw him quickly looking at my legs and then at me fully. Hmmm, interesting, I think he likes what he sees.

The lunch was pleasant and full of conversation, something I soon discovered is one of Walter's gifts. There was lots of laughter around Walter discussing golf and suggesting that he and Jim get a foursome to play Bandon Dunes, an original links golf course in Oregon. I jumped in and asked what about women since I love the game and play whenever I can. Walter looked at Jim with a smile, then said, "Sure, women can come," but you could tell there was some secret man code that implied this outing was for men only. Then he said, "You know we play eighteen holes each day, sometimes thirty-six, for the three days we are there but of course you probably play back to back all the time." He looked at Jim and smiled again knowing that most amateur golfers rarely play back–to-back rounds. I shot back that we women could always play a round, shop, and then play another round. Walter replied, "Oh don't get me wrong, I like playing with women, just not golf." That evoked even more laughter from everyone.

After we acknowledged the donation and thanked Walter, we got up to leave and Joyce suggested that Walter walk me to my car because she recently had knee surgery and couldn't get around without some discomfort. Now mind you, we are in broad daylight at a shopping plaza so we all looked puzzled, but Walter, the consummate gentleman, said of course and off we went. Little did I know at that time that Joyce wanted us to have some "alone time" because she was not sure we clicked during lunch". We walked and talked about everything and nothing until we got to my car, a little macadamia brown Porsche. I asked him if I could give him a ride back to his place but he declined. Then, I asked him what he was going to do for the rest of the day, but he was noncommittal so I just drove off thinking there was no interest on his part.

I drove home and as soon as I entered the house the phone rang, it was Joyce. "So, how did it go?"

I said, "How did what go?"

She replied impatiently, "What do you think about Walter?"

"He's okay but not very interesting," I said.

Joyce seemed surprised. "Oh? Is he going to call you?"

"Well, he didn't ask for my telephone number so I guess not," I replied.

"What? Wait a minute, I will call you back," and she hung up. She called Walter to ask him why he didn't ask for my telephone number and he said he thought it was a business lunch. Joyce replied, "Well, Kay would like you to call her." Then she called me back and asked if it was okay to give him my telephone number, and I answered yes. Then she called Walter back, gave him the number, and said call her. Whew!

"Hi, um, this is Walt. I am going to try to make the golf tournament and I thought if you aren't busy we could have lunch or something after the tournament."

"How about dinner?" I asked. The golf tournament was on a Saturday and I knew I would be exhausted so I suggested we meet on Sunday. He agreed and I said I would make a reservation, which I did, in his name at a local restaurant that has music.

Walter did play in the golf tournament, and after the round, we all gathered for the Chrystal Awards Luncheon. Once again Joyce intervened by selecting a table and arranging the seating so I was sitting directly across from Walter to ensure that we could get a good look at each other. Because I was the chairperson for the event, I had a lot of responsibilities and was running around making certain that everything was moving smoothly. When I finally sat down I was exhausted and quietly said, to myself, "I wish I had something to drink." When I turned around in my chair there was Walter with a glass of iced tea. He simply smiled and returned to his seat. After the luncheon he came up to me to say good-bye and to say he would see me tomorrow. At that moment I thought what a quiet man but what presence he has. I just felt him all around me.

Of course Joyce called to ask what happened and I shared with her that Walter had called and that he was sending a car to pick me up for dinner. "What? Sending a car, just a minute I'll call you back." Joyce called Walter to tell him that he couldn't send a car to pick me up. Sure enough a few minutes later I got a call from Walter saying he would pick me up around 5:00 p.m.

It was a lovely dinner full of easy conversation. After dinner we walked around a bit, Walter loves to walk, and again we had light conversation, nothing that I remember, but pleasant. He brought me home and said good night.

Joyce called the next day. "Well, how did it go?" I told her it was nice but I don't think we clicked. He is not really my type and I think I am a bit glitzy for him. However, he did say he was coming in the following weekend and if I did not have other plans perhaps we could have lunch or something.

What is it about men that they can't commit or at least come right out and act interested? What does "we can have lunch or something" mean? I think the coy thing does not work well for me. The danger here is that I could have missed out on the best thing that has ever happened to me if I had tried to interpret Walter's interest. So, I guess the message is to follow your own feelings. If you are interested, stay focused and stay open to possibilities. Instead of shutting down the relationship before it has a chance to evolve, look at the half full glass instead of the half empty glass of possibilities.

"I Don't Email, Talk on the Phone, Show Affection in Public, or Make Long-Range Plans"

Walter did come to Phoenix for the weekend, and this time I drove to his place. There are great restaurants in the Biltmore area. We decided to walk through the underground tunnel that connects one side of Camelback Road to the Biltmore Fashion Park on the other side. It was a wonderful evening. After dinner we walked some more and then headed back to his condo to get my car. When we reached the underground tunnel, no one else was there except a young man playing songs by Stevie Wonder on his harmonica. Without a word, Walter took me in his arms and we danced. It was magical! Afterward, I slipped my arm into his and we walked to his condo, still without conversation.

Walter invited me up to sit on the pool level of his building. The views overlooking Phoenix at night were beautiful. A full moon, stars, and the city lights at night added magic to the evening. We sat next to each other and shared our first kiss—light, sweet but full of feeling. He had just returned from Spain so he was running low on energy and I could tell he was very tired so I simply said I better get going. He agreed and we shared another light kiss. Then, while we were going through the door, he said the strangest thing, "Just so you know, I don't email, talk on the phone, show affection in public, or make long-range plans." Although I was caught by surprise I was thinking: *Really, are you the same person who just danced with me in a tunnel? Are you the same person who leads teams of top executives in leadership?*

After I got my thoughts together, I replied, "Let me ask you a question, if you were starting up a new company or opening an office, wouldn't you spend some time making certain that it is moving in the right direction?"

He smiled and said, "Call me when you get home so I will know you are safe."

I drove home a bit bewildered about his comments and then I thought we'll see about that. So I called expecting to have a bit of a conversation because of our kiss but all he said was, "Glad you made it home safely, good night," and hung up. I think I held the phone for a few seconds in disbelief that he hung up on me. Who is this guy?

I do know in many of the seminars that I have conducted nationally over the years that men and women communicate differently. This is nothing new but when you are in a relationship or trying to develop a relationship, in most cases, women are the more talkative, always wanting to discuss and "feel" a sense of clarity. In our thought process we always want to know "do you understand what I am saying?"

In my experiences men want to solve a problem, get to the bottom line, they are not big in exploring just for the sake of exploring without seeing a path for a solution. I think men are the same in personal relationships as they are in business. That is why I asked Walter what would he do if he were starting up a new company or opening an office. He didn't respond. I now think that it was not because he didn't have an answer. I think he thought it had no relevancy to our situation. He was giving me the conditions under which he would be involved with me, and I wanted to know why. Walter was not ready for a why because what he said is what he meant, nothing more. He was defining how he felt at the moment. In other words, he was expressing the bottom line, the solution. He had no desire to discuss anything else. When I think back on how bewildered I was when I called Walter to let him know I arrived home safely but also expecting to have some conversation, it all makes sense. To Walter, a conversation was simply not necessary or productive. The evening was over. It was great, good night.

How many times have we heard our girlfriends express that their significant other has no feelings? As hard as you try to tell him what is important to you he doesn't get it.

You are engaged in thoughts and feelings, and he is engaged in tangibles. He can't wrap himself around thoughts and feelings. What do you want? He does not want the description. He wants the what.

I remember being in a coaching seminar and the consultant, to make a point about how people seldom are clear about what they really want, asked several people to come up on the stage with him. When each one stood next to him, he asked one simple question, "What do you want?" Not one person could answer right away. I think no one ever asks us what we want because we are so busy focusing on taking care of our immediate needs. This is not to say that men don't have wants. On the contrary, I am simply amazed at the deep thought men put into responding to a survey about what qualities they find attractive in women, which I will discuss later. I think men are just more private with how they express their wants, particularly if they are also looking for "The One."

This is just a thought, but perhaps men think they are giving you what you need not what you are expressing as a want. Well, what's the difference? When you need something, it is essential to your existence—water, food, shelter, clothing, and love. When you want something, it is like a fringe benefit—it is something after the needs have been met. Wants come and go but needs are fixed. I want you to love me is different than I need you to love me. Walter often says to me, "I want you because I need you."

I'm Thinking About You

Are You Thinking About Me?

Isn't it strange how people have one opinion about you and all of a sudden you find yourself trying to conform to that opinion? It is as though you want to be the person that they want you to be because you want them to like you so much that you are willing to give up your identity. All the while you know that your real identity will burst out no matter how hard you try to suppress it. It is like trying to put a lid on a container that is too full. The more you press on the lid, the more the contents seep out. You are who you are and certainly after a number of years you should want to be comfortable with you, yet you find yourself in a constant state of wanting to improve, which I guess is a good thing. I once said that my deceased husband made me want to be a better person. His words still echo in my soul, "Always take the high road."

The phone rang and it was Walter sharing that he was coming in on the weekend to take care of some business. Oh my, three weekends in a row. Earlier he had shared with me that he comes to Arizona perhaps two or three times a year. However, he did say that he just purchased a new condominium so perhaps he plans on spending more time here. Who knows?

Walter is so exact, he sent an email suggesting that he or his assistant would contact me with his plans for an extended weekend visit to Phoenix. He would say something like, "This is just a suggestion of ideas subject to how we feel or decide at the moment." And then he would add, "Pray it all works and that we have this time together." I discovered then that Walter is very spiritual.

I invited him to attend a luncheon with me. I purchased the tickets and this was a pivotal point in our relationship because it was the first time we went together to a public event that many of my friends attended. Then Joyce, my friend who introduced us, was having a birthday party and Walter asked if we should attend or at least drop in for a little while. I called him and left a message. He was not home. Little did I know at that time that he really doesn't answer his phone, so I emailed him. I shared that I thought we should attend given the fact that Joyce introduced us. He agreed. Walter called later that evening. Mister I-don't-talk-on-the-phone talked for two hours before hanging up. He kept interrupting what he was saying with, "I don't talk on the phone," and then continued our conversation. I could tell he was really surprised with himself.

That weekend proved to be a semblance of what life is like with Walter—one event after another, moving constantly so that when he leaves, I am exhausted! The weekend started with me picking him up from the airport on Thursday evening. We had a light dinner and then I drove home. We attended the luncheon on Friday and enjoyed being with each other. We had our picture taken, a photo that is now one of my favorites. On Saturday we drove to Sedona, a lovely little town north of Phoenix.

The drive was beautiful and we talked nonstop all the way. We explored each other by asking the typical questions: Tell me about your family. What type of work do you do? What's your favorite type of music? Do you like movies? Walter said he was sort of a low-key under the radar kind of guy. Quiet, unassuming, unpretentious. Right. Low-key and quiet as I listened to him talk endlessly. I admired the car we were driving in, a midnight blue four-door Aston Martin, and he laughed and said he fell in love with the car while watching a James Bond movie. But basically he defended himself by sharing that although he loves to talk, he seldom talks about himself. I found that to be true as I found myself rattling on about me.

I further learned that Walter, although not shy, was a bit uncertain about how to act around me. It wasn't until later in our relationship that I discovered he was uncertain because he really hadn't dated other women after his wife's death. I found it absolutely amusing that he asked his son what he should do only to receive an embarrassing response, "You're dating?" His son revealed to me that he didn't know what had come over his dad. He said, "My father doesn't talk about dating, about sex, not with me."

I understood Walter's standoffishness even more when he shared a story about going to a corporate dinner event and meeting different women who knew he was widowed. One woman when leaving the event came over to say to Walter how much she enjoyed meeting him and extended her hand to shake his. She pressed a napkin with her telephone number on it into his hand while smiling seductively. She was delighted when Walter immediately followed her out of the event anticipating that he was going to ask her out. Instead he held out the napkin innocently and said, "I think you left this by mistake." The woman was indignant and Walter didn't understand why she was so upset until he relayed what happened to a friend who laughed hysterically at him and his naïveté.

The art district in Sedona is wonderful, scores of art galleries with unusual and beautiful artwork. We went into one store, Exposures, and saw a beautiful bronze sculpture titled *Waiting for the Bus.* I fell in love with it. Walter was in the process of decorating his new condo so I suggested that he buy it, but he didn't express any interest. We had only been dating for a month and although he would ask for my opinion I knew when to advise and when to step back. So I stepped back. Besides, he had an interior decorator who seemed to know what Walter wanted and would make suggestions to which Walter would simply say yes or no. I on the other hand wanted to know other color possibilities, durability of fabrics, and comfort level. I got the impression that the designer was happier when I was not around because Walter, although adamant about what he liked, was easy to work with and didn't go back and forth like me. Anyway, the statue was so perfect, I wanted him to buy it for his place, but he said he would wait. It was also very expensive so I understood he wanted to make certain it was the right piece.

After exploring several galleries and a few stores, we stopped for lunch at a lovely little restaurant by a brook. I took our first "selfie" and loved it. Walter doesn't like to take pictures. I think it is because he freezes and the camera catches an uneasy subject. He said that for security reasons he shies away from pictures since one could always be traced by the background of pictures, and in his line of work that would be a breach of security. What does this guy do? I, on the other hand was thinking, I must teach Walter our family secret when it comes to pictures. When every member of my family from the youngest to the oldest sees a camera, they know it doesn't matter how unprepared or what the mood, they know to strike a Hollywood pose in seconds with a generous smile showing teeth every single time. Even my dog knows how to pose. As soon as the picture is taken, gone are the teeth and smile and back to whatever mood we were in before the camera flashed.

While having lunch I asked Walter what month he was born in and he rattled off the month, day, and year immediately. No one ever asks what year you were born in because then the other person would expect me to tell them the year, and we all know that women don't like to tell their age after thirty. On top of that, I discovered that he was younger than me. Little did I know that Walter already knew everything about me. I think he had access to personnel records through his work so I am certain he had all my information, credit scores, finances, and work history before he even asked me out. Yikes! Also, his son and daughter-in-law googled me. Googled me—are you kidding me? I checked Walter out for myself based on the criteria my father gave to his three daughters: Never date a man with wrinkled clothes or rundown heels. It means he does not care much about the order of his life. I checked Walter's clothes and shoes out the first time we met. I on the other hand was googled! I observed him for myself and I knew I wanted to spend more time with him.

We returned from Sedona with a new appreciation for each other, at least I did. There was something about Walter that kept drawing me to him. Each time we talked and each time we were together I felt completely mystified by him. I now use the term *enchanted*. I sent him an email, "I like the way you talk with your hands, I like your eyes, I like the way you put your hands in your pockets while walking around observing everything; nothing goes unnoticed. I like the way you stand close to me and . . . I loved dancing with you." It has only been a little more than a month since I met Walter and he has sent me an email just about every day! Slowly, very slowly Walter and I are unfolding our personalities and revealing who we are to each other. I now think, as I reflect on past relationships, something that everyone says: Don't rush it. Let it unfold slowly, naturally at its own pace. Something is happening, something wonderful, and something that we have no control over. What is this?

It's the Fifth Day Since I Said I Love You!

I remember the exact day and time when Walter said, "I love you." We had just returned from dinner and we were standing in front of the fireplace in my home in Scottsdale, and he just said it—calmly, quietly, and without any reservation. I was so surprised that I blurted out, "You are not in love, you're just infatuated."

He said, "No, I am in love with you."

What could I say, he was so sincere and all I could think is what's happening here. So without really thinking I blurted out, "Walter, I think you should date other women. Take each one out twice and then decide if you are really in love with me or just infatuated."

I told Joyce, the matchmaker, what I said to Walter and she was just livid. "Are you crazy? Why would you tell him to do that? Don't you know women are asking me every day why I introduced him to you and not to them? You go back and tell Walter to forget that."

I said, "No, I will not. I think I am the only woman he has dated seriously, meaning more than just an occasional dinner date, since his wife passed and I don't want to be the woman who sees him through his grief then loses him to someone when he is ready for a serious relationship to come into his life."

However, I didn't need to tell Walter to forget what I said. Walter told me he had no desire to date anyone else. He knew exactly how he felt. I asked him, "How are you so certain you love me?"

He said without any hesitation, "Because I have been loved all my life. God loves me, my mother, my father, my wife, and two sons loved me. I know love."

I was flabbergasted as I sometimes am when Walter fires out one of his pearls of wisdom. I didn't know that kind of love. I always believed in God, but as a child I wondered if He loved me. My early childhood was not easy. I didn't always feel loved and therefore found it difficult to know or show love, not having experienced it. As I grew to adulthood I recall understanding the concept of love and family only through television programs such as *The Adventures of Ozzie and Harriet* in the 1950s. I mean, I had a mother, father, and two sisters, but divorce and violence were more prevalent. My sisters and I did not feel unconditional love growing up, and on the contrary, we found only conditional love.

When I married, I mimicked the concept of love and family based on what I thought was how a family should be, how a wife should be, how a mother should be. If truth be told, I learned those roles so well that I could easily have won an Academy Award for my portrayals. Those portrayals became my reality and I liked what I created: a home, a loving family, and children who I adored and who were loved unconditionally.

So I guess my question to Walter was not about his knowing that he loved me but the profound impact his declaration of love had on me. He loves me but do I love him? This is not a simple question because love can be defined in multiple ways and levels. You have a love for your friends, family, and even organizations. You have a deeper love for your children and your spouse. The *American Heritage Idioms Dictionary* defines love as a "variety of different feelings, states and attitudes that range from interpersonal affection to pleasure."[1]

To me love is giving without asking for anything in return, simply to make another person's life more pleasant. It means to accept pain from another understanding that your love is unconditional whether you experience pain or pleasure. We experience this love with our children, siblings, and spouses. Love is never ending. Love is simple, not complex, it just is. The more I think about love the more I see what Walter has experienced. I am loved. That love is my arsenal that allows me to do all the things that I do because regardless of the outcomes I am loved.

---

[1] love. Dictionary.com. *The American Heritage® Dictionary of Idioms by Christine Ammer*. Houghton Mifflin Company. http://www.dictionary.com/browse/love (accessed May 26, 2016).

I've known the love of my children, sisters, and friends. I guess I have known love. I experienced love at different intervals and saturations than the love Walter has known, which has been constant throughout his life. The love he has known is deep and not superficial but rather what Eric Fromm, a prominent German social psychologist, spoke of: "Immature love says: 'I love you because I need you.' Mature love says 'I need you because I love you.'" Hmmm! Walter said to me once while we were talking about loving people, "You don't love what you think a person will be, you love what that person is right now. No more thoughts on changing him but rather accepting who he is." John Legend writes it beautifully in his ballad "All of Me," "Love . . . All your perfect imperfections."

Sexuality, Sex, and Swag

How do you discuss sex when you have grown children who probably think you have been abstinent since they were born? But how do you leave out something so beautiful and perfect when you are in love? We enjoyed kissing, holding each other, and basically just being close. But as the days turned into months we still were quite reluctant about being intimate. Of course my girlfriends asked, "How's the sex," and I would always say, "Not yet." Soon they were asking, "What's wrong?"

I would answer, "Nothing, we just aren't there yet."

"Is he gay?"

"No."

"Does he have problems," asked amid raised eyebrows.

"No, we just aren't there yet." I didn't explain that it had been quite some time since I had sex and I was feeling a bit apprehensive about it.

Who would believe me? After all, my girlfriends and I had discussed at length our sexuality in terms of being sexually attractive. We all agreed men like a woman who is sexy without being vulgar. We believed that being sexy has nothing to do with the act of sex itself but everything to do with what leads up to it. I believe it is how you dress, classy but not prudish; your physical appearance, well-groomed, clean hair, manicured hands and feet; your disposition, a warm and inviting smile and attentive eyes; being physically present and focused; and most importantly, not being loud or offensive. This is sexy! You donned these attributes to be attractive to the person you want to be with, to the person you eventually have a relationship with, to the person you want to have sex with.

My doctor even asked when was the last time I had sex. Good grief! Obviously I know that our sexual life is an important part of our physical well-being, but I was surprised at her multiple suggestions to remedy my situation. I asked her what I should do. "Engage in self-satisfaction or hopefully within a select relationship," she replied, and then continued, "It is natural and necessary for your happiness." I had never thought about it that way. After all, you have to have a partner who you feel you want to be intimate with and for some time now I was dating but not wanting to have a relationship with anyone.

Then, along came Walter. One evening Walter was leaving after sharing how much he cared for me and we embraced and then kissed. Before I knew it, I was leading Walter to my bedroom. I was nervous and wondered with each step what on earth did I think I was doing. He probably thinks I do this all the time. Now I have to take off my clothes. Is he going to do anything? No, he just watches me! Good grief. This is a mistake but I can't back out now, he is taking his clothes off and getting in my bed. We reached for each other as naturally as we could pretend and it just happened, slowly, naturally, and with a lot of "trying."

The next morning no one was speaking and I thought something was wrong so I said to Walter, "Are we having an argument and I don't know about it?" He didn't say a word at that point but after breakfast he came over to the couch where I was sitting and sat down. He talked about our first night together very analytically trying to explain how he felt that he had disappointed me, but I knew I had disappointed him. After all, I was very seductive and put on a good front and then could not deliver. I used every cream, gel, lubricant that I could think of and still entry was painful and difficult.

Back to my girlfriends, "What to do?"

"Oh no," was their response. "Did you try this? Did you try that?" They were no help. Back to my doctor who simply said I needed to practice. Egad, my sister's favorite expression, what is she saying? Get lubricants and practice? Okay.

I couldn't bring myself to go to a pornography store so I ordered a few "items" online, but they turned out to be more than I wanted to deal with. Then one day while waiting to pick up a prescription at my drugstore, I wandered around, and there in aisle 5 plain as day were a number of lubricants and sex toys you could actually see to determine which ones you might like to try. So here I am at my age standing in a drugstore placing all kinds of items in my basket, sheepishly going up to the cashier hoping no one will look into my basket or worse yet, bumping into anyone I know.

The next time we spent the night together we were at Walter's condo. He must have known my uneasiness because he had lubricants, I had lubricants, and we had messy awkward sex. But the next morning, we looked at each other with the type of unspoken words that only people in love use and we made love, real love, gently, beautifully, full of touching and kissing everywhere. The kind of love that fulfills you completely, leaving you exhausted and glowing. After that morning we spent many days, afternoons, nights, and unexpected moments loving each other knowing that we were each other's comfort and joy. From then on, our emails became more intimate describing our need to see each other and to express how amazed we are with how our relationship is evolving both emotionally and physically. "Hi, I miss you. You must stop thinking about me when you wake up in Virginia. I feel you . . . I woke up at 3:15 a.m. my time in Arizona and I loved it."

Oh my, five emails from the person who specifically said he did not email or talk on the phone. It seems there are not enough ways to communicate because we have so much to share—how his day is going, how my day is going, what happened yesterday, what is going to happen tomorrow. Finally, someone who cares about my existence, my day, me! I don't understand how I am feeling but I do understand how wonderful I feel.

Every day is something new with Walter. Today, beautiful roses instead of orchids sent unexpectedly. He likes to do that instead of celebrating birthdays or other holidays exploited to enhance the profits of the capitalistic market like Valentine's Day. Walter likes to give gifts just because. Whatever his rationale, it seems he is always thinking of something special, such as the time he asked me about my golf game. I told him I am a person who is continually trying to enhance my game, in other words I manage to stay on the golf course without embarrassing myself too badly. His response was, "When is the last time you changed your clubs?" I told him I didn't play well enough to change my clubs frequently. He replied, "The next time I am in town we are going to get you fitted for a new set of clubs, you'll see your game improve immediately." Whew!

Walter came in town for the weekend and I got a new set of Ping clubs. I told him that I was not financially ready to buy new clubs and he just smiled and then told the salesperson to get a ladies golf bag to put them in.

This is corny, who does this? More roses and a card that reads, "Will you be my sweetheart?" Next, a scarf from Hermès with a handwritten note that reads, "This scarf is a Thanksgiving gift to you from me. Thanking God for you!" Who needs a holiday to receive gifts? Right now I am living every woman's dream—I met a man who can and will do anything to make you happy. But wait, step back. . . What am I saying? Walter is more than gifts and words.

What is it about this man that makes my heart race whenever he comes toward me? He has incredible eyes but he is not tall, he is average looking, he does not have, oh what is the word my girlfriend uses all the time, I know, *SWAG*. *Swag*, as defined by Google, where else: "Can be a noun, adjective, a verb and an all-purpose expression of agreement or endorsement."[2] Walter does not have swag or does he? Googling will help you find anything you want, and I found that some people think

---

[2] swag. *Old Person's Guide to Swag* by Adrian Chen. May 23, 2011.

that *swag* is a replacement for *cool.* Others think *swag* is *cool* with hip connotations. The one I like is, "Swag is how you dress, walk, talk and carry yourself." (President Obama has been described as having plenty of swag.)

Definition of swag: The way you talk, dress and how you carry yourself.[3]

Walter is not cool but he has presence. Is that the same as swag? Back to Google: According to Dictionary.com, it is "*the ability to project a sense of ease, poise, or self-assurance . . .*"[4] Umm! I guess Walter has plenty of swag. He is an impeccable dresser who wears European tailored clothes, shoes, and accessories—most selected by a personal stylist. Even his casual attire is perfection. His walk is comfortable, business-like, direct, neither hurried nor slow. His talk is his gift—he is nonstop until he engages you completely. I witnessed this myself when I once listened to him talk to the most obnoxious man who talked about himself nonstop. Midway during the conversation I noticed that the man was quiet and listening attentively to Walter. I asked Walter what on earth did he say to him. Walter smiled and said, "I redirected his comments from trying to impress me by talking boastfully about himself to talking about what his aspirations are and how he might accomplish them." Walter has swag, the quiet under the radar, as he describes himself, type of presence. He is just all around you, into you, consuming you. Walter has swag!

---

[3] http://www.dailywaffle.co.uk/2013/08/tips-for-men-how-you-can-dress-with-swag/

[4] presence. Dictionary.com. *The American Heritage® Dictionary of Idioms by Christine Ammer*. Houghton Mifflin Company. http://www.dictionary.com/browse/presence (accessed May 26, 2016).

The Sprinkling of Love Dust

I have two sisters. One lives in Orlando, Florida, and the other lives in Phoenix, not too far from me. Both my sisters are great people. The one in Orlando has a heart of gold and would do anything for you. The one in Phoenix is very attentive and tries to take care of everyone. When I told my sister who lives in Phoenix about Walter I think she knew immediately that I was really taken with him. As a caregiver, her solution is not to leave anything to chance so she asked me to invite Walter to our family Thanksgiving dinner. Although all of the family would not be present, my daughter and Walter's son live in Atlanta and my other sister as shared earlier lives in Orlando, the majority of my family would attend.

Because of past experiences with family and friends, I could picture my Phoenix sister planting a St. Joseph statue upside down in my yard. Oh no, that's for selling your house quickly. Perhaps she'll plant calla lilies. Our girlfriend mentioned how much she loved calla lilies, and the next thing she knew my sister was in her yard with her gardening hat on, tools in tow, and planting calla lily bulbs. What good will that do? I'm trying to impress a man and she already planted beautiful calla lilies lining the entrance to my home. Perhaps she'll create a love potion in one of her famous signature cocktails. She is good for that, but we would all have to drink it. I know she is going to do something. I just don't know what.

Walter had an afternoon meeting in Virginia on Wednesday and would fly in Thursday afternoon and meet me at my sister's home. I was on pins and needles waiting for his arrival because this is the first time he would meet my family. When the doorbell rang I raced to the door but my sister beat me to it and motioned for me to step aside. When she opened the door, Walter was standing there and before anyone could say hello, my sister sprinkled him with a glittery substance and said hi, you've just been Highgatetimized. Highgate is my maiden name and her husband swears that once you have been Highgatetimized, which is involved with a Highgate, you will never be the same.

Walter was a big hit. Everyone seemed to like him, except my son. My niece-in-law whispered, "He really seems nice." My sister and her husband smiled approvingly, and my grandchildren seemed indifferent but looked at him and then ran off and played. My daughter lives in Atlanta so she was not there to provide me with her wonderful assurance that everything is just fine. I wanted Walter to feel comfortable and he said he did. But Walter is such a conversationalist that it is difficult not to like him. At one point I walked into the dining room and Walter was sitting across from my son. Oh no! My son interviewed my previous husband with pen and pencil in hand.

What is with this boy? Later I asked Walter what they were talking about and he just smiled and said, "Let's just say that I answered all his questions including the ones he didn't ask." Okay, that's it I'm through.

It's December and I continue to be amazed by what is taking place in my life right now. Is it the newness of our relationship that keeps me wondering what this is? I keep thinking to myself I must be near death because everything is so perfect. How do you respond to someone who sends you orchids? But wait, there is more. The orchids are accompanied by a note that reveals the most tender side of a man. Expressions that most men don't reveal, and maybe that is what is so amazing: This man chose me to express his feelings and captured my soul. He shared that he sent orchids instead of roses because of their longevity and that they represented two attributes of our relationship, wholeness and love. Geez!

Some would say that making a woman happy is impossible. If men only knew it is actions, not looks, not words, nor promises but actions that can win any woman's heart. A woman wants to feel special, desirable, and captivating. She also wants to feel safe and that she can trust a man, meaning that no matter what is said or done, his love will overcome anything and he will always be supportive. In essence, the secret of making a woman happy is to give her what she really wants: love, security, and trust; that special feeling that she is the most important thing in his life.

You would think that at best you can only provide these attentions at the beginning of a relationship knowing that the intensity will soon fade. Walter has taught me something very simple. By giving continuously you slowly begin to receive continuously the same attentions with the same intensity over time. That is, if a person enjoys receiving but only gives back occasionally, the attentions fade; the relationship deadens and falters. But if both people give these attentions reciprocally, they are intensified, deepened, and cherished as each gives to the other for no other reason than to make the person in their life, as Walter says, essential to his existence.

Ten Qualities Men Find Attractive in Women

A man like Walter is not after any woman. His position alone could provide him any woman he wanted whose intentions may or may not be genuine. Most think that women are attracted to good looks, money, and power. While that may be true at first glance, as my father used to say, "Good looks can get anyone through the door but once inside, now what are you going to say?" A man like Walter needs a woman who can accompany him to a variety of venues both formal and informal. He needs a woman he would not be afraid to leave alone to hold an intelligent conversation when not in his presence. And he needs a woman who understands the necessity of dressing appropriately. That would be me!

These are all the things I knew were important, but still I decided to ask some of my male friends what qualities they found attractive in a woman. Then I realized that maybe I should also ask the most important man in my life what qualities he finds attractive. Walter replied, If I wanted to score some points, I would say just list everything about you."

I smiled and then said, "Now tell me what you really think." Surprisingly he named many of the same qualities my male friends shared with the exception of one. My male friends listed this quality as one of the ten qualities they look for in a woman. Some listed it first and some listed it midway through their list. Walter identified this quality as the overarching quality that sums up the total essence of a woman.

I decided to expand the number of men I wanted to survey so I emailed approximately fifty additional requests to men of all ages, races, marital status, and religions. I received responses from twenty-eight men. So I guess I could say that I conducted an informal survey to create a database after posing the question "What qualities do men find attractive in a woman?"

I want to share with you that all of the men who completed the survey were very thoughtful. They took their time and gave me specific qualities they wanted in a woman. When I talked to some of them I was surprised with how serious the single men took the request. One shared with me that from the first time he takes a woman out he subconsciously assesses her. He made it clear he is never looking seriously but rather described it as the more qualities a woman possessed, the more attractive she becomes and the more involved he becomes. That makes sense, but what I found complicated is if there were negative qualities that emerge along with positive qualities, the relationship is prolonged until the positive qualities outweigh the negative ones. But if the negatives outweigh the positives, the relationship is ended. The respondent said that this process is nothing he thinks about consciously, it just is. So here are the top ten qualities given in the order of importance listed by the respondents.

Compassion

Although having compassion was identified ten times in the informal survey, it is the most difficult quality to discuss. Having compassion is often aligned with empathy, and that is partially correct. Empathy is often experienced first before compassion. Empathy is a passive emotion that simply explains how a person can identify emotionally with another person's suffering whereas compassion requires a person to take action to assist or eliminate the suffering. As an example, a person can feel genuine sorrow for a friend whose family member is addicted to drugs. He or she may have had a similar experience with a loved one and therefore can identify with the pain the friend is going through. In other words, the person is empathetic to his friend's suffering. It is not unusual for the person's feelings to evolve into compassion. When this occurs the person not only empathizes, that is, identifies and feels the emotional pain his friend is experiencing, he also wants to take some form of action to assist in the alleviation of the pain. Thus, empathizing is identifying emotionally without any additional involvement. Compassion is empathy with action. When compassion is typically defined, it is within the context of feeling another person's suffering or pain.

I believe the respondents in the informal survey thought of compassion within a broader context. They identified several qualities they found attractive in women such as being kind, generous, loving, warm, and caring. These are all attributes of a compassionate person. I believe that a woman can demonstrate all of these qualities in small and large every-day circumstances. As an example, a woman can listen to her man describe an embarrassing event that took place at work. Because she loves him and feels his discomfort, she might help him debrief the event to help him see why he felt embarrassed. Together they can determine what steps he can take to overcome his embarrassment. This is showing compassion. She is caring by listening to him. She is giving by helping him debrief the event. She is showing a loving spirit by being there for him.

On a much larger scale, a woman can marry a man with children. She is empathetic to the hostility that the children demonstrate because of the marriage. She is action oriented, compassionate, when she sits down with her husband to discuss what they should do to help the children accept the marriage. She lovingly gives more time and energy to the children to help them talk about their concerns. To give of oneself to meet the needs of another is a noble act.

When you combine giving with loving you are providing others the ultimate gift that God requires of us. These scenarios demonstrate compassionate love. I ask again, why is it that men would place such great emphasis on wanting a compassionate woman? I think because they view compassion as encompassing all the attributes of love, the most powerful emotion we have.

Pleasing Appearance

Your physical appearance is your first introduction. A quote attributed to Will Rogers sums it up this way, "You never get a second chance to make a first impression." One of my single male friends asked for my advice about a woman he met online. He shared that after a few telephone conversations they decided to meet for coffee. They chose a restaurant midway between their homes and set a time. He dressed casually not wanting to overdress since it was just coffee, and she turned up in a very provocative skin-tight dress. Of course you want to look your best, but a tight revealing dress is a little too suggestive for an afternoon coffee date. Am I old-fashioned?

I have seen women and young girls everywhere at all times of the day in dresses that they had to constantly pull down to cover their behinds. At the same time, I notice the men looking at them. So what do you think? I am going to ask my girls. My girlfriends gave a lot of responses such as, "Men like sexy women" and "She just wanted to show off her best assets." But let's just cut to the chase. If "Pleasing Appearance" is the quality identified the most in the survey, could a provocatively dressed woman fit in that category? Maybe. What is pleasing to one man may not be pleasing to another. Which led me to ask, what was the woman thinking about? Clearly her need to dress provocatively is what she feels is most attractive to men. So here is the cliché, a provocative-dressing woman must find a man who wants a provocatively dressed woman. So the quality "Pleasing Appearance" is a personal preference that can only be defined by each individual man. After all the conversations I had with men and women, my takeaway is that your physical appearance is one way to attract similar people.

The most important thing to remember is you feel good when you look good. When you see a person who takes care of their physical looks, which includes their hair, face, body, clothes, and shoes, you can be pretty sure you are dealing with a person who cares about the impression she makes in her personal and professional life. Your physical appearance, therefore, is very important because it is the first thing a person sees when you meet. It doesn't matter if you have known someone a long time, if you meet her looking like she just completed a marathon and fell down, you are going to ask, "What happened?" We try not to be judgmental because we know looks can be deceiving but in reality, physical appearance is a pretty good indication of how a person perceives herself and the influence she has on the world she lives in.

Spiritual Commitment

At the beginning of the introduction on what qualities men find attractive in women, I said that most of the respondents and information I read identified several qualities that emerged as more important than others. There was only one quality that was hard to define because the respondents identified it in several ways such as God first, morality, spiritual compass, and, Walter's first response, spiritual commitment. As I struggled to understand what the respondents wanted to convey, I thought their responses were similar in content just conveyed in different ways. After doing some research, I chose to identify that quality as spiritual commitment.

The University of Minnesota's Center for Spirituality and Healing and Charlson Meadows website (*www.takingcharge.csh.umn.edu*), suggests

> *"Spirituality is a broad concept with room for many perspectives. In general, it includes a sense of connection to something bigger than ourselves, and it typically involves a search for meaning in life. As such, it is a universal human experience—something that touches us all. People may describe a spiritual experience as sacred or transcendent or simply a deep sense of aliveness and interconnectedness."*

I understand this but I wanted to understand more deeply what the respondents meant. After pondering all the responses, Walter's description lingered with me. He said a woman is most beautiful and more desirable when all of the other qualities are embedded in her spiritual commitment. He explained that everything he does is directed by his faith, his trust in God. He said it doesn't matter what religion you are or what you believe in, rather it is important that you believe and have faith in something bigger than yourself.

Spiritual commitment is not something that you can see and touch, it is deep within you. It guides you in everything that you do. So when Walter lists spiritual commitment as a quality, he is assessing if a woman believes in something other than herself. A woman with spiritual commitment is loyal to that which she believes in. A loving spiritual commitment in the best of circumstances is reciprocal. You commit to other people the same way you commit to God, and God commits to you the same way He commits to other people. Therefore, a woman who is spiritually committed to God will be spiritually committed to her significant other, and their love for each other will grow and be strengthened by that commitment.

Confidence / Independence

This was a difficult category. The men in the survey seemed to combine the terms confident, determined, fearless, independent, and self-motivated all together. I decided to focus on confidence and independence since they coexist with each other. A confident woman is usually an independent woman and vice versa. What is it about a confident woman that men find so appealing? Is it that she seems to know where she is going and exactly how to get there? I think this is only part of the intrigue. A confident woman seems to be in control of her life and if she makes mistakes, she simply accepts the consequences, gets up and starts all over again. Each mistake she makes is a learning experience she discusses as the driving force needed to reach her goals. And there it is, she has goals. A confident woman is focused on her accomplishments and how each one can help her develop a skillset that will ultimately define who she is and what she is.

Men view confidence as powerful and even sexy. However when a woman or any person makes it clear by their body language or spoken language that they have no self-confidence they are actually saying I need someone to direct my life or I might make a complete mess out of it. We all know these people. They are our relatives, friends, co-workers or others who have come to trust that we will listen to their needs and if possible help them to solve their problems. Some are quiet and simply don't get involved in making decisions that impact their lives. Others bring you their problems and feel relieved that you will listen and act on them. Having self-confidence leads to self-esteem, which leads to independence.

While watching Joel Olsteen an American preacher, televangelist and author one Sunday morning, he discussed the power of turning away from people who are in a constant state of dependency on others to meet their needs. I learned that you can certainly help others as much as you can but not to the detriment of your own peace and happiness. He called them peace stealers, people who pull on you emotionally and when you relinquish, you deny yourself peace. I thought of this when I listen to the men share with me that independence in a woman is admirable. It signals a person who is in charge of her life and not emotionally dependent.

Most confident independent men admire women who are independent. I think I was caught up in the old adage that men like women to be dependent on them, to be needed by them and to be the providers, food gathers. I know you are thinking is she for real? What time capsule has she been hiding in. Well, my interviews revealed that men still want women to need them. The problem is, in this economy women have become providers as well as men or they've become the main provider in the relationship. So the trick is to show your independence without letting your man think that you don't need him. Or, better yet, to convey that you have needs that only he can meet that are beyond financial security. I find independence to be a funny thing. I think when men say they want an independent women to need them they are actually saying I want a women who can stand on her own and not depend on me for her happiness. Independent women don't need a man to complete them; they are a complete package all by themselves.

Pleasing Personality

The respondents want a woman with a positive personality. One respondent wrote, "No drama." Others listed they want an emotionally stable woman. I recall talking with my son about dating when he said, "If women only knew what a turn off it is when a woman tells you about her traumatic childhood or degrading past relationships. A first date is the wrong time to delve into negative history."

The respondents defined pleasing personality as a happy person, someone you are glad to see because they make you feel good and indicate that they are happy to see you by their smile, a quick hug, or a warm greeting. A woman with a pleasing personality is pleasant, you want to be around her because she has a way of making everything seem better. She carries herself in a positive manner and you expect positive meaningful conversation instead of gossip. She is a good listener and shows how she admires your thoughts while expressing her own views in a constructive manner and in such a way that you are drawn into her way of thinking. But she is also flexible and with all sincerity compliments your views as she embraces them, making you feel very good about yourself.

There are a lot of articles and books online that discuss the attributes of a pleasing personality, many more than I was aware of until I began this journey. It is amazing to me that the respondents, some professional and some laymen, identified a pleasing personality as an important quality and here it is blasted all over the Internet. I think I am surprised because I consider myself well-read and have held leadership positions, taught leadership skills, and know that a pleasing personality is a trait most successful people have. Or do they? I don't think we notice it until we come up against people who either have a pleasing personality or don't have a pleasing personality. What I do know is that I am grateful to these men who thought deeply about what they wanted in their ideal woman and I thank them for that. Here are a few of the hundreds of articles I found online for your perusal. "10 Ways to Improve Your Personality" by Z. Hereford, "Pleasing Personality—25 Key Traits" by Napoleon Hill, "Transform Yourself into a Pleasing Personality" by Ravi Mahajan, and "Attributes of Leadership—A Pleasing Personality" by Kerwyn Hodge.

Enjoy Sex

I think just saying that a man wants a woman to enjoy sex is very superficial. That's not what I think men want to say. I think they want to say that they want women to be present while having sex. Men can have sex with women, but what about women having sex with men? To be present means to contribute and to be a partner while making love. It just makes common sense that if you both are contributing you both will enhance your enjoyment. In an article entitled, "Why

So Many Women Don't Enjoy Sex as Much as They Could" (Salon.com, February 27, 2015), Amanda Marcotte writes, "The problems start with how we define sexuality. Male sexuality is generally understood in terms of what men want from sex. Female sexuality is too often defined in terms of what men want from sex." Marcotte then writes, "But women are more likely to focus on being desirable instead of focusing on their own desires." Instead of playing the submissive role, women can let their partners know they have wants and needs and more importantly guide their partners in how to satisfy them.

I think too often women find themselves wanting to be sexually attractive and begin to lose confidence as they age. Cellulite, vaginal dryness, and the worst culprit, sexual desire, begin to play havoc psychologically. I love an article I ran across written by Pamela Madsen, "Three Unspeakable Truths About Female Sexuality," where she writes that there is so much taboo around female sexual desire, "It amazes me and stuns me every time I trip over another fate that is keeping women in a place of uncomfortable sexual endurance rather than a place of sexual pleasure." The three unspeakable truths are "1. You just can't have too much lube." It makes all the difference between painful sex and utopia sex. "2. Women can suffer from sexual boredom just like men." All I can say is variety is the spice of life, experiment! "3. Many woman's sexual experiences could be remarkably improved by learning how to receive pleasure as opposed to developing skills on how to give pleasure." How unfortunate that the mind-set of most women is making certain the man has an orgasm. Let's make a shift as Madsen writes and assist women in becoming "receivers instead of doers" of their organisms. Women can enjoy sex as a contributing partner, and men will feel the difference because they both will feel completely satisfied. So to all the men out there, sex is not just for you, it is also for the woman in your life. If you want a sexual woman, open up and learn how to give insurmountable pleasure. You know the old cliché, the more you give, the more you will receive.

Integrity

Out of the ten qualities men find attractive in women, integrity surfaced as one of the top five. Why? Integrity is a virtue. A woman, or anyone for that matter, who exhibits integrity is a person who is sought after in every aspect of life. Integrity means you are a person who can be trusted, a person who will always do what is right and just. As I write these lines, I sit silently asking myself what really is integrity? I think it is something only you and God can see. When a woman or any person exhibits a profound sense of integrity, which is what is right and wrong, not in a judgmental way, but with a sense of what you believe to be morally right. Integrity is something that I don't think you can learn. I think you are born with it.

Integrity is something that develops over time into this personification that makes up your being. What I mean is that as a child you learn right from wrong and as you develop you soon understand the decisions you make are based on those fundamental principles that make up your moral code. Your integrity is the foundation of your moral code. Other attributes like honesty, truthfulness, worthiness, and sincerity all emerge as part of the filter through which you manage your life.

When others view you, they see your character. Most would argue that character is also a born trait. I don't think so. Unlike integrity, as you mature you can mold your character to fit the acceptable view of others. No one will know because you have mastered presenting an image that you think others will admire. Over time the image you present may become your enhanced character shaped by experiences that influence your behavior. Good experiences impact your behavior in positive ways and you are programmed to repeat the behavior. Behaviors that cause bad experiences cause you discomfort and you therefore eliminate those behaviors. Herein lies the problem as you interact with people, unless you have a strong sense of integrity, your behaviors adapt like a chameleon, changing to fit your surroundings. This is an admirable trait particularly for survival purposes. However, will anyone ever know who you are, what your position is, or what you believe in? The question ultimately becomes, who are you? I love a quote I read by Barbara De Angelis. She writes,

> *"Living with integrity means: Not settling for less than what you know you deserve in your relationships. Asking for what you want and need from others. Speaking your truth, even though it might create conflict or tension. Behaving in ways that are in harmony with your personal values. Making choices based on what you believe, and not what others believe."*

Have Interests, Goals, and / or Hobbies

The most frequently asked question when you meet someone for the first time is what do you like to do? Everyone wants to know what you are interested in. Most interviews include a question about your interests, goals, and hobbies. When I interview people, I ask the question because it gives you more personal information about who the person really is. A simple response such as, "I like to go to art museums," gives the person asking the question some insight into your artistic side, what you value, and your appreciation for learning new and different things. When a man asks what are you interested in, he really is asking who are you and what kind of life do you live? Is it exciting or boring? How are your interests, goals, and hobbies aligned with mine? What are you passionate about? What are you focused on? If you have well-versed answers to all of these questions it means that you are living a full and interesting life. You are intriguing because you focus on living not on existing.

Men fall in love with women who are focused on living, as I say, dramatically and out loud. On the other hand, if you shrug and say, "I don't know, lots of things," this response could imply that you are shy about talking about yourself or you really live a quiet uninvolved life. Nothing wrong with that except as it is with an interview, you want to impress the man and ensure him that he won't be your only interest, goal, or hobby. The operative word is *only*. He can be the focus of your life, your being, but not your only interest. That could be a bit creepy and could lead to obsessiveness.

When I was dating, I met a man who asked me what I liked and I went on and on with a litany of things I love to do. When I finished I settled back and asked him what he liked to do with great anticipation. I remember almost his exact words because he said, "He goes to the library twice a week and watches the news channels and sports programs on television." I think I stared at him for what seemed like a few minutes not really believing that he left his apartment only twice a week. What about church? What about going to the grocery store? What about a jazz concert? After I finished staring at him and he finished staring at me, our nonverbal communication said to each other, "Not a match."

Sense of Humor

There is not much to say about wanting to be with a person who is full of laughter and always sees the glass half full instead of half empty. No one wants to be around *Saturday Night Live* fictitious character Debbie Downer, the person who can take a wonderful moment and turn it into a tragedy by providing negative comments that sometimes have no relevancy. I know a person like that. I was telling a group of friends about this wonderful trip I had taken and mentioned that the tour group I was traveling with prepared a gourmet meal outdoors under the stars every night. Everyone oohed and ahhed and wanted to know about the food and the setting, but this person's only comment was how many bugs and flies did you have to kill? Although this happened some time ago, I still remember it as though it were yesterday.

There are studies that indicate that humor is connected to health. The more you laugh the more you feel uplifted, stimulating your mind and body and thus relieving pain, depression, and other feelings of inadequacy. It is even suggested that humor can prolong your life. I am not certain of that, but I can attest to humor making life more bearable. When my husband was dying of prostate cancer, we tried everything during his last months to change his depression. What we found worked best was comedy. I can't say enough about *Ghostbusters* (1984) and the television series *The Jeffersons* (1975–1985). We often found ourselves in stitches watching these reruns even though we knew the end was near. As it relates to the respondents wanting a woman with a sense of humor, friends often call friends when they are feeling down to give them a shot of humor or to pull them away from their own pity party. Feeling good outweighs feeling bad every time. People like to be around happy people, people who are lighthearted and well meaning. Men in particular don't want to spend their time around angry, ugly, mean-spirited people. If you feel bad, stay home!

Joy to the World

I just finished decorating the tree and decided to hang a few more Christmas bulbs. I dropped one and it shattered. I thought about what Walter said—putting up a tree is hard work. It is hard work, with a little disappointment, breaking the bulb. But, it is also so much joy. As I stepped back and looked at the tree, I was just full of joy that I finished it. Everything is hard work. As I listen to Walter comment on his schedule, he works so hard but it brings him joy. A marriage is hard work but the memories are full of joy. My life has been full of hardships and lots of sadness, but I have experienced so much joy. Walter is part of my joy and I am just a little nervous because our relationship is so easy. Maybe it is not hard work at all because everything hard is behind us, leaving only joy.

I have thought on many occasions and shared with my friends that perhaps my life is coming to a close because everything, I mean everything, is so peaceful. I am living the life most women dream of. My bills are paid and my children and stepchildren are doing well with their own families—with some obstacles but nothing they cannot handle. Even if they are confronted with a difficult hardship I am blessed to be in a position to provide assistance. The real blessing is my grandchildren who surprise me every day with their intelligence and creative spirits. My sisters, although sometimes estranged, are a part of the fabric that makes up my life, and in my heart they can never be replaced. I have a lovely home and an adorable little Shih Tzu/Lhasa Apso. who gets me up and keeps me busy. I have great friends and belong to several organizations that I am proud to be a part of because of the work we do in our community. And, I have always found a church or place to worship that provides me a sense of spiritual peace and nourishment.

Our minister recently shared that he has on occasion visited with a person who is terminal. He shared that he expected to consul the person and of course the family. But what some terminally ill people say to him is that they feel peace, a very calming peace, and are not afraid to die. When my father was dying, I remember him sharing with me that he was ready to go. He was at peace with how he had lived his life. He said that he certainly wished there could be some "do overs" but all in all he accepted his faults and always tried to do good in every phase of his life.

So, has my time come and now I feel at peace because as the Apostle Timothy wrote, "I have fought the good fight, I have finished the race, I have kept the faith (2 Timothy 4:7)? Whoa! Is this about joy or am I getting ready to die because I feel so much joy and peace? Of course, I have learned about joy from my children, children-in-laws, grandchildren, and just about everyone, but if you want to know, google it. So I did and I found an article posted online that I think is very appropriate to place right here. In an article written by James

Baraz and Shoshana Alexander (2012, https://experiencelife.com/article/7-ways-to-experience-more-joy/), they write that joy is a choice that anyone can make. Both authors suggest that there are seven suggestions that I think are so simple but yet so life changing that I am including them here because now I know why I feel so much joy.

1. *Imagine Happiness*

   I do have a pretty positive outlook on life. You know, the glass half full versus the glass half empty concept. I spent most of my younger life thinking about being a part of a loving family, a life that had no abuse, and one where I could become anything I wanted as long as I worked hard and stayed focused. I had to have rose-colored glasses to make my world more beautiful than what it was. I simply decided to live a life I made up, that I imagined, instead of the actual life I was living. That tiny decision carried over into my adult life so I always saw every person as having a gift to be discovered and that every opportunity was waiting for me just around the corner.

2. *Memorize Happiness in Your Body*

   Sometimes you can get so carried away with fantasy that you can't see reality. I couldn't memorize happiness because I didn't know what it was. But I could pretend and emulate happiness from afar. As long as I kept people at a distance I could protect myself by pretending to live in a world of happiness when situations became too unbearable. As I grew older, with age comes wisdom, I can now recall moments of happiness that I did experience and feel joy when I remember them and thus want to recapture that feeling for the here and now.

3. *Reframe Your Fate Positively*

   Earlier I talked about the glass half full versus the glass half empty. How we view the world we live in has a lot to do with how much joy "we let into" our lives. If we have a negative view of the world, then very little joy can emerge. Associated with a negative view are sadness, frowns, ugliness, wrongness, and depression. And from these unhealthy views, spring hatefulness, bitterness, and jealousy. Before you know it you are wondering what on earth life has to offer to you. You and only you have the power to change your view of the world, but it is a difficult pattern to break. If your life is consumed with a negative view, how do you create a change? This seems silly, but to me you focus on happiness! With a positive view comes, laughter, happiness, beauty, and more likely than not a new network of people who want to be around you. Change is hard but be determined to take small incremental steps. Think about one good thing that came into your life last week. Increase it to two good things, then begin to look for the good things that happened to you in a week. Can't find any? Then, make something good happen on your own. Reframe your fate by changing how you view the world. It really is a beautiful place.

4. *Strategically Diffuse Worry*

   I don't think any mother can diffuse herself from worry, but you can learn how to control it. Worry does nothing unless you have a plan to eliminate the cause for your worry. By creating a plan, you are strategically diffusing worry. Don't worry for nothing, worry for something. When you worry for something you can identify the source of your worry and now you can either act on it or just continue to worry. As my daughter-in-law would say, "How's that working for you?"

5. *Experience the Bliss of Blamelessness*

I haven't conquered this yet. I'm stuck. Somehow, *it's your fault, it's his fault, it's her fault, it's not my fault* all seem to creep in my head and come judgmentally out of my mouth. I do want to experience the bliss of blamelessness, and I think sometimes I have. Let's just say old habits are hard to break and I am still in training. I am not a Debbie Downer, and I seldom throw a pity party or feel I am worthless whether I make one mistake or many mistakes. My childhood taught me how to take charge of myself, my mistakes, and move on. It is blaming others that I need to improve on.

6. *Let Go of Feeling Busy*

Walter had a hard time with this when he first retired. He was always creating a list of things that had to be done on a given day. Now, I know many people have a list but I don't. I just don't need a list of things to do after working for thirty-seven years where every hour was consumed with things that had to be accomplished that day. In my world some things get done and some things don't get done. I am in no hurry except when I have a deadline or when I am going to the grocery store, then I want a list.

7. *Seek the Good in Others*

This one is easy for me. I always found the good in others. I always find something to admire about everyone I meet. My philosophy is that everyone has a gift, all you have to do is look and you will find it. I was often

> accused of attracting the most undesirable people simply because I saw something special in them. But in my defense, not that I need it for what I believe in, there is good in everyone. I often found that some people are willing to hide who they are because they are anxious to be liked by everyone, so what you see is a shell of a person instead of a person full of gifts they have submerged for defensive reasons.

Wait, I have not embraced all of these suggestions as much as I want to but they certainly will go on my list of changing me for me. I know who has embraced all of these suggestions. Yes, that's right, Walter.

166 Emails Later

Would You Like to Go to Church with Me?

When I was dating Walter, I attended a wonderful church that I was very involved in. Approximately fifty people attended, perhaps more on some Sundays and less on others. One of my closest friends and I taught Sunday Bible Study. We really enjoyed co-teaching with each other and rotating our class monthly so we each had an opportunity to learn as well as teach. The camaraderie and preparation provided a very rich and deep experience for us as well as for the people in our Bible Study Class. Many of us have become dear friends. We don't see each other as frequently as we used to, but whenever we do, we greet each other warmly and with love.

Because our church was so small, everyone knew everyone by name and noticed when you were absent. If you were in need, you found almost the entire membership reaching out to you. So naturally if you had friends, relatives, or just invited someone to attend, everyone knew they were your guests. One weekend I asked Walter if he would like to go to church with me on one of the Sundays I was not teaching, and he said yes. He picked me up and I took him to my church. It was the first time I invited a man to attend as my guest. When he helped me out of the car, I noticed he had a Bible in hand. My girlfriend taught on that Sunday morning. When we entered the assigned room for our Bible Study, Walter came in and immediately made his way to the back of the room. He encouraged me to sit where I normally sit, close to my friend so I could offer any assistance she may need. The person not assigned to teach that Sunday was responsible for getting the materials from storage and passing them out. When I left to get the materials and returned to the room, Walter took them from me and passed them out and then returned to his seat. I watched him as we moved through the lesson. He was fully engaged and taking notes. Wow!

I didn't know how spiritual Walter was when we first met. He talked about his church but not inordinately. He knew I taught Sunday Bible Study but we only talked about it casually. After Bible Study, I took Walter to the main area where the service was held. Of course everyone was looking, "Kay brought a man to church." During the service once again Walter took out a small index card and began to take notes on the sermon. I was impressed. Hmm, Walter was scoring all kinds of points. After service everyone wanted to meet him because as I shared earlier I had never brought a man to church with me before. We had not been in many social settings together so I was always in a one-on-one conversation with Walter. This was the first time I could stand back and watch his easy casual way of talking with people, drawing them in by asking about their lives and loved ones. Of course my guys (I call them *my guys* because they are the men in my life who I have great respect for and I know they have respect for me) in my Sunday Bible Study were all over him and the verdict was unanimous, Walter was labeled a great guy.

My church is important to me and certainly I have high regard for most of the people who attend. The guys in my Sunday Bible Study were also part of the golf ministry that I belonged to so their opinions were also important to me. I could see them looking Walter over with great scrutiny. Guys know guys and I knew they would not hold back any criticism if they sensed anything that was not what they considered to be on the up-and-up. That's the great thing about friends, they tell you like it is. You can't see anything because you are excited about having a man in your life that looks to be by all accounts a respectable thoughtful guy. That's why I always look for an approving nod from my family and friends. After all, if things go well he could become a part of your family and a part of your circle of friends.

A Red Flag

Oh my! Everything is wonderful, I can't seem to find anything wrong with Walter and believe me, I am looking and just waiting for a red flag. It's cold outside and Walter is in town attending a board meeting. I was not sure if he would have any time for me, but as it turned out, after he got settled, he called and said he wanted to see me and I was very excited. Perhaps I would meet some of the people he works with, after all, our relationship has taken on a new dimension, we are in love! So when he called to say that I didn't need to drive all the way up to the hotel lobby because he would be waiting for me at the entrance to the resort, I thought that's a bit strange. He said he wanted to take a quick run before meeting with me because the meetings were so intense. Wouldn't he want to change clothes and take a shower after jogging?

Walter was standing in the entrance to the resort that opens to the drive about a half-mile from the hotel. He was sweating profusely and also coughing. What in the world was he doing. The temperature is in the low 30s outside and he is setting himself up for a very bad cold. We had a quiet evening because he started really coughing. I gave him some medicine and he finally went to sleep. The next morning I drove him to the resort and was making my way up the long drive to the hotel entrance when he told me to just let him out here and he would walk the rest of the way. What? Something is wrong! I decided to drive him up to the entrance anyway, but he insisted very adamantly that I stop the car and let him walk the rest of the way. So I did, but my women's intuition started working overtime and I became furious. Red flag!

After all, in my world there are only two reasons why a man does not want to be seen with a woman. One, he is embarrassed to be seen with her. Two, there is another woman somewhere in the picture. There could be a third reason, you don't want anyone to know about your personal life. But no one needed to know what our relationship is—I could have been anyone dropping him off. So, two reasons still exist. He leaned over to give me a kiss but I turned away, I was puzzled and angry, very angry . . . no hurt is a better description of what I was feeling. This is a situation you have to take to your girls who will clearly see what is really happening here. So I called them one by one. *It's another woman . . . Perhaps you are overreacting . . . Call him out on it . . . If you really love him, accept his explanation and let it go . . . It's another woman.*

Walter called the next day but I wouldn't pick up the phone. He next sent an email that was very revealing . . . he was angry. Isn't that just like a man to "flip the script" as the kids say? His email was so intense that I include it here because I can't rewrite it and keep the emotion true. It started with,

> *"What, are you kidding me? I did not kiss you because when you let me out of the car, you leaned away. I get*

it you are obviously mad or hurt by the whole idea of dropping me off at the turnaround versus the lobby. I am hurt, almost destroyed that you would even think, or bring up, that there is some other woman and to label my actions as a man thing versus a person that you have some knowledge of really hurts. Look I am truly sorry, sick, mad, disappointed and in the middle of serious issues at work today and not able to talk with you about this. I am not going to play this game; I am going to call you, so please pick up the phone so I can at least hear your voice as you share how hurt you are. Please know that all of this time, I was concerned about you catching my cold even a little, because when we last talked you said you were not feeling well, So please pick up the phone."

Yeah, yeah, yeah . . . Another woman.

Second email:

"Okay look I am more calm and less emotional and therefore more reflective. We are both strong-willed people and were involved in the heat of the moment that obviously led to misunderstanding or interpretations of actions, or the lack of actions, that then led to hurt feelings, which lead to further actions of response based on those interpretations, i.e., this string of emails and rushed phone calls. I regret that our time together ended that way but I truly look forward to our make-up time together in a few weeks and even phone calls and emails until then.

"Now to answer some core issues, (1) I am not ashamed to be with you I just did not want to deal

with explaining anything to that audience about my personal life at that time; (2) I truly appreciate someone really caring about and for me when I am sick, it is still very hard to accept so I will error on the side of not allowing you to help, it is a work in progress; (3) I love you and want to struggle with discovering all the ways that are possible through these and other experiences; and (4) I got emotional when my love for you was, as I interpreted it, questioned or challenged by you or anyone. I only ask that you love me and pray for me; these are tough times."

Oh my, why do I always look for the negative first? What was really going on with Walter? And then it hit me after reading his email. He was not ready to share his personal life with his colleagues. Hmmm. Walter lost his wife; I lost my husband. Several things happen when you lose a spouse. First and foremost, you grieve in a variety of ways that leading experts define as stages that move from denial, anger, depression, hurt, etc. One is mindful of family and friends who are also impacted by the loss of a spouse. I have been widowed for several years. But when did Walter lose his wife? I quickly google the obituary and knew immediately why Walter acted so strangely in terms of not wanting me to drop him off. He thought it was too soon. He was not ready to explain to his family and friends, let alone business associates, that he had fallen in love with another woman so soon after his wife's death.

But what is too soon? Doesn't it depend on the circumstances? I knew he loved his wife dearly, but I also learned that she had been ill for some time and in her final months, she was in a coma. I felt his pain as he shared with me that he placed his wife in a nursing facility with twenty-four-hour care. His intentions were to sell their home and move into the apartments connected to the nursing home so they could be together, but she died before all the arrangements were finalized. So what is too soon?

If you don't know google it, "What is the proper period for mourning?" I could be reading forever with the wide range of responses, but generally a year to two years seems to be the most acceptable. Walter was alone for twenty-two months before the matchmaker, Joyce, decided that we needed to get together socially. Was it still too soon for him? I do know, having experienced loss personally, what is enough time for one person is not sufficient for another. What is dangerous is when you mourn to be mourning instead of mourning to provide time to heal from a painful loss. I have my answer, Walter is feeling guilty. He thinks it's too soon.

So, Walter will know when he is ready. He is a man worth stepping aside for and allowing him space to do whatever he needs to do to enter a new relationship without feeling any guilt. Most importantly, he is extremely sensitive to how his son will react to his father falling in love with another woman. As I continued to see more clearly, I realized that Walter and his son were all that was left of his family. He lost a son several years earlier and now his wife, which means his son lost a brother and his mother, and Walter was all he had. Oh my!

PRAYERS

Although I can talk a good game, I realized that loving Walter is complicated—a term he frequently used early in our dating when I would ask him about our relationship. Giving him the space that he needs but also wanting more from him when he obviously cannot give any more at the present moment is complicated. However, there are those moments that begin to define your relationship and pull you closer together even while you are struggling with defining who you are in another person's life. All couples share highs and lows that help to define them as a couple. You need him for something or he needs you for something. How you respond or should I say if you respond, increases the idea that you are special, valued, needed because someone actually places value on your opinion. Awesome!

As an example, Walter's work is demanding so when he asks me to pray for him, I feel honored that he thinks my prayers are what he needs to make it through a rough time. I remember sharing with him that I prayed for him and thought of him throughout my day. I think God made Walter into who he is so he could be all that he could be for others. I am thankful to God for Walter because I know that all the people he comes in contact with know that he is a fair and just man. In my heart I believe that when God is in your life, nothing will come to you that you cannot handle. The relationship is so complicated that I give up all control and trust it will evolve in ways that we never thought possible.

The Bentley

I was having some issues with my car and began thinking about buying a new one. Walter asked if I wanted to go car-shopping and I said yes. I thought I might look at another Range Rover or a Jaguar. One weekend in March when Walter flew in for the weekend we drove to a section of the city that has multiple dealerships all in the same location. Walter said he had to take his car in for a brief inspection and that we could kill two birds with one stone. So we took his Aston Martin into the Penske dealership and then we walked around looking at different makes and models. After asking me what kind of car I was looking for, he proceeded to tell me why that particular car was not the best deal for me. So I thought to myself, *fine I will just come out here by myself and look for the car I want, such as that beautiful emerald green Jaguar even though it was a bit more than I could afford.*

So we went back to Penske's to pick up Walter's car. Parked outside of the showroom was a burgundy metallic Bentley Flying Spur. I only know the name because Walter smiled and said, "What about that car?" which made me look at it closely.

"Oh sure . . . a Bentley," I replied.

"Let's take it for a test drive," he said.

"I don't think so. There is no way I can afford this car," I said. But off we went, me in the front driving, Walter in the passenger's seat, and the salesperson sitting in the back giving me driving directions.

The car was so big that you could lie down in the back and front. I felt like a little girl driving my parents around. It had every luxury appointment you could think of. Back massage, heated seats, cooling system for your drinks, hidden compartments for all sorts of things including a hidden panel to place your umbrella. It rains a lot in England where Bentley is manufactured, so in an English luxury car, a place for your umbrella is an elegant touch. After the test drive Walter asked me how I liked it. I looked at him and said it was great. He said good and the next thing I knew we were in the showroom talking with Walter's salesperson and he was asking me what kind of car I had. I told him I owned a 2004 navy blue Range Rover and had a balance on a macadamia brown Porsche. He said good, this is what we can give you on those cars toward the Bentley.

While we were having this conversation, with my mouth open—in amazement,—there was a football game on. I don't know who was playing but Walter was fixed on the game. He asked his salesperson to write up the car. I whispered that I couldn't afford this car and he smiled. He told me I didn't have to and took out his checkbook. When the paperwork arrived Walter was still looking at the game. He looked at the paperwork and then back to the game. At one point, he let out a shout and I thought *oh my, how much does this car cost?* But he was responding to a fumble made by one of the players and then calmly wrote out a check for the entire amount of the car. When the salesperson asked him who should the title be made out to, without a pause, he gave him my name. I was in shock!

The first person I called was Joyce who screamed and kept saying, "No he didn't." Then I called my sister and her husband in Phoenix, and she said, "Is there any doubt how he feels about you?" They just kept laughing and then she said, "You know this only happens in romance novels and with movie and hip-hop stars and gangsters." *Gangsters?*

I drove to my monthly women's meeting and after the meeting many of the members surrounded the car. They were in awe with the beauty of the car. There was no pretending, none of us had ever been inside a Bentley. I drove one group of members around in the parking lot and then another group until everyone had a turn. It was so much fun. They took pictures and texted them to their husbands, boyfriends, and other friends. I think their spouses and significant others are going to hate Walter.

It is so important to have friends, good friends, who are happy for you and want to be a part of your happiness. You can tell who is really happy for you and who is envious. I don't have time for evil. I only wanted happiness and was thrilled that my real friends came out that day to rejoice with me.

The Look of Love

Some people say that when you are in love you have a certain glow about you. So many people have told us that we just glow. It didn't happen once, it happened on several different occasions. We were shopping and a salesperson behind the counter leaned over and with a smile said, "You two are such a beautiful couple." Another time we were attending an outdoor jazz concert and a man came up to us and said, "The two of you are the best-looking couple in this entire event," and there were hundreds of people there. But the most moving comment was when Walter and I were finishing lunch at a local mall. We always sit side by side instead of across from each other. We saw a woman looking at us and acknowledged her with a smile. She was leaving the restaurant and then turned around and came over to us. She said she had just gotten out of a terrible relationship and had given up on finding happiness with another person until she saw us together. She said, "The love you show each other gives me hope."

Her words made me cry. I told Walter that I was so happy and I always wanted to know if he was happy too because the way he makes me feel is indescribable. I ask myself all the time, is this real? I feel like I am in a dream, the perfect love relationship. I said to him, "Please don't stop loving me."

"Never," Walter replied.

Love attracts people to you. All of a sudden you notice people noticing you and it is such a different feeling. People smile and acknowledge silently that the two of us have something special and they see it. In addition, men are everywhere but my eyes see only Walter. The same is happening to him whether he is aware of other women or not. When a man is in love, women flock to him. In his case I always knew it would happen but much subtler because of his position. That's why I wanted him to date others to make sure of his feelings. Now I know how he feels about me, so I am good.

Walter once shared that in corporate America the biggest mistake men make is getting involved with people on the job. Top executives are judged by how they handle their personal lives as well as their professional lives. My father thinks a man is judged by four things: his wife, his house, his car, and his shoes. I get the first three, but his shoes? My father instilled in me to always look at a man's shoes. If his shoes are scoffed and his heels are rundown, it makes you wonder how he handles his affairs. Is that anything like how a woman cares for her feet? Bad feet equal bad personal and work habits, I'm just saying!

So, I share my dad's philosophy because Walter is very professional, he would be very careful not to jeopardize his standing as he sought to move up the corporate ladder. Entanglements lead to mistrust by superiors. So in his mind getting involved as a married man or even playing the Casanova role as a single guy is just not worth compromising the hard work it took for him to achieve his position. There is something else, Walter is a Christian and his moral code would never allow him to be devious in any way. I had another close male friend who fell in love with another woman while married and decided the relationship was not worth losing his wife, children, and the family home. He explained the home is where the sacrifices were made, children's memories lingered, and in essence the very foundation of the family. He never told his wife but he did tell a close friend who advised him to stay in his marriage and never talk about it again.

The Timeline

Little did I know that others were watching the development of Walter's and my relationship with great anticipation. Even Joyce's mother, who is ninety-five, chimed in sharing she met and married her husband after knowing him for four months. Whoa Ms. Juanita, we are just now comfortable with saying I love you and dating for just about six months. Once again, how long is long?

All kinds of timelines were surfacing, timelines that we did not plan for or were even aware of. Walter shared that he would no longer accept or describe himself as being two months' behind my thought process. He told me that he was actually one year and nine months ahead of me. What does that mean?

He said, "I know for sure what is important in my life: I am striving to have an improved relationship with God. I am dedicated to ensuring my grandchildren's holistic education, and I desire to spend the rest of my life with you. I have faith that all of these things are being worked on and being developed or maturing in my life. But I don't know how, at what pace, or where the journey will unfold. I am dedicated to making these things happen. I am generally pleased with where I am with each, but I need to strive harder to have greater progress with my relationship with God." Oh my, timelines.

Sometimes I can visualize Walter philosophizing. He seems to get great pleasure out of talking openly and deeply about issues without censoring his thoughts. Right when I think he is still not sure what he wants or where we are in our relationship he blurts out that he wants to spend the rest of his life with me and that things will merge at a point in time when he no longer lives in Virginia. What does that mean?

I didn't believe Walter when he first said he loved me and now he is indicating some permanency in our relationship, but I don't see him behaving that way yet. When I confront him he simply says he has faith, quoting the Bible, that "faith is the assurance of things hoped for, the conviction of things not seen" (Hebrews 11:1) as the state he discovered he is in not knowing how the rest of his life with me will unfold but believing it would. Okay, what do you do with that? I hate when I don't have a rebuttal!

It's Complicated

We sat in the parking structure outside of Saks at the Biltmore Fashion Park almost in the same area I parked when I first met Walter. I was trying to determine exactly where our relationship was going. He would expound on his love for me and how he has faith that we will be together, however, what does that mean? I told Walter I felt like I am always on the peripheral edge, almost in his life but not quite. We will be together someday, but when is someday?

We were well into our relationship and we spent quite a bit of time at his condo or at my house almost every weekend. He left some slippers, workout clothes, and shoes at my house. I always carried a little bag with a change of clothes and some toiletries. On one of our visits, I decided to bring some things and leave them in his condo. While I was placing them in a drawer, Walter said, "What are you doing, trying to move in on me?" He wasn't joking and I did not see a smile. Where is the love? What happened to "I want to spend the rest of my life with you"? Oh yes, I forgot . . . someday. So I packed my things back up very quietly and took them home. After I left, Walter called to ask what happened to my things and I told him that I had no intention of moving in on him and that the next time I bring my things to leave at his condo, he would need to ask me.

So there we sat in the car not having our usual light, funny, loving conversation. I said, "Walter, I feel like I am placed in a compartment and when you are here, you take me out and we have this wonderful time together. Then when you leave, you put me back into my compartment and that's that. What type of relationship do we have? Where is this going? Should I date other people? Do you want to date other people?"

Walter was quiet and reflective, the way he is when he is pondering what he wants to say. But this was different. His hands were sweaty and I actually could see he was very uncomfortable. I thought to myself, *Well, well, well, Mr. Cool isn't so cool today. Where is our relationship going?* Walter replied, "I don't know. I haven't thought about it. I am not ready for anything serious I don't think?"

"What! Dare I say you said you had faith that we will be together for the rest of our lives?"

I am thinking, *umm, you don't know?* After an hour we finally got out of the car, both of us very solemn. I didn't get the answer I wanted and he was a nervous wreck. I wanted him to say that we are in an exclusive relationship even though I knew we were. I wanted him to say let's move in together. I didn't know the details, I just wanted him to confirm what I was feeling and that is, there is no one else he wants to be with.

Wait a minute, maybe he doesn't love me. When you don't know something, the simplest thing to do is just ask, so I said, "Walter do you love me?" No answer, just staring at me. The stare that says what do you think? It reminded me of a time when we woke up and I was in his arms and said "Your pajama top is wet but just in one spot. What kind of sweating are you doing?" There is that stare. Again, what do you think?

"You drooled on me," Walter finally said.

"I what?"

"You drooled on me."

"I slept on you with my mouth opened and drooled on you?" Ye gad!

Then he added, "You snore."

Oh no, I am completely devastated. After my shower, I put on my night cream and lotioned my entire body, using a special lotion for my hands and my feet. I put on a lovely gown and went to sleep looking perfectly beautiful. Now I find out that I sleep with my mouth open snoring and drooling on him. What must he think? Walter is in love with me and I am in love with him, and we both know it. But with that being said, where do we go from here?

Meeting the Kids

I suppose, one place to start is to take the big step and meet the families. I told my family about Walter and I will save their remarks until later! But I am sure this is difficult for Walter. Once again I understand his hesitation. Walter had two sons, he lost one several years prior to the loss of his wife. Now there is just his son, his daughter-in-law, and two grandsons. Walter is all his son has now that his mother and brother are gone. How do you tell your son that you are in love with another woman when the death of his mother and brother are still so painful?

Some things seem so trivial but so meaningful to both of us. As an example, both of us have a child who lives in Atlanta, my daughter and his son. So off to Atlanta we go to meet each other's child. Although sensitive, we thought it through and decided that for our first visit it was too much to bring the families together so we booked a hotel in between the two and decided to meet his son first.

When we arrived I felt a little nervous, but Walter was so nonchalant that I soon calmed down. We knocked on the door to a lovely brownstone located on an exclusive side of Atlanta and his son who was very warm and charming met us. His wife was pleasant but not overly warm. She was expecting her first child and was really quite adorable. We all just stood in the middle of their living room talking. No one asked if we'd like to sit down or if we would like a glass of water. Although they were friendly, I felt scrutinized and uncomfortable again. But that's their job, to protect their father against harlots!

Walter wanted me to take a tour of their home although I didn't want to intrude. But Walter insisted so we went up the stairs and down the stairs until we got to their bedroom, and that is where I drew the line. We made our way down stairs where the most amazing thing happened that just reaffirmed how important Walter and his son are to each other. Walter was talking about something and making a gesture as though he were holding a golf club and hitting a golf ball, he does that often while he is waiting or contemplating something. Very quietly, his son came up behind him and wrapped his arms around him and kissed him on his check and said, "I love you Dad." It was such a heartwarming moment that I nearly cried. After a few hours we left and went back to the hotel.

The next day we visited with my daughter. I felt so much more comfortable. My daughter is one of those people who although extremely beautiful is just very down to earth and oh so loving. She greeted Walter with a warm hug and I immediately felt at ease. My three grandchildren came in and they were their usual inquisitive but polite selves—not showing their real personalities that consist of harassing each other and jumping all over me. My youngest was on the floor playing with his LEGOs and before anyone knew it, Walter was stretched out on the floor next to him. They talked with each other and my grandson kind of lay next to him quietly talking. My daughter told him to move, but Walter told her he was fine. Later, I asked my daughter if she knew that the senior vice president of a Fortune 500 company was lying on her floor playing LEGOs with her son? Walter will never know that I fell more deeply in love with him that weekend. It wasn't until I was reflecting on our visit did I realize that his youngest son and my son have the same name and at that moment it hit me that my grandson's name is the same as his oldest deceased son's. Wow!

I said I would revisit my kids' reactions when I told them I had met someone special, so here it goes. I have my son and daughter and a stepson and stepdaughter. My stepson said, "I am so happy for you, it's about time you found someone for you. Just let him know that I don't mind spending a couple of years in jail if he acts ugly toward you." My stepdaughter is very theatrical, so she screamed "Yay! I am so happy for you." My daughter said, Great Mom, but don't get pregnant! My son said, "Your time has passed, why don't you just be content with your kids and grandkids?" Ouch. I stared at him for a few moments and then turned around and cried.

As I look back on our children's reactions I now know that both sides had experienced upheaval and wanted no more of it. Walter and his family experienced the death of his wife and a son. His son lost a mother and a brother. My family experienced a divorce and the loss of two good men. Wow! We should have thought this through more carefully but we were so happy and forgot that our children were not experiencing the same emotions. They only experienced loss. And now, they may see our relationship as another loss to them personally.

I remember once after I remarried trying to share with my daughter how my love for her could never be diminished. She was just eleven and I was lying on her bed with her in my arms telling her that the heart was a wonderful place. It never replaces or forgets those that you love, it only expands and finds room for everyone. Sometimes you have a hole in your heart that no one can fill, but you learn to live with that loss by concentrating on those who are still with you. And that is what Walter and I are doing. Our hearts are full of holes that can never be filled, but our hearts are much bigger and full of new loves that allow us to cope with our loss.

VANCOUVER

One week away from everything. I can't believe Walter is actually taking a week off work to go to Vancouver. We are both excited. This is our very first trip together and I think we were both a little nervous about how we would get along for an entire week 24/7. Personally, I am only good for four or five days at the most. We bonded beautifully. There are no other words to describe it. There were small things that I had to get used to such as Walter paying for everything. I had money to spend on small gifts and tokens that I wanted to purchase, but he quickly took over no matter what and paid. I soon learned that Walter likes being the man. And, I love it.

There are so many things that you learn about a person when you travel: sleeping habits, morning habits, eating habits, exercise habits, fun habits, and developing together habits. I was thinking I should give a person space, that's what I need, but I found myself wanting to be with Walter all the time, and I could feel he felt the same way. We would get up and plan our day. It wasn't long before I discovered that we liked many of the same things. Although I am not an outdoor person—spending the night on the ground in a tent or worse yet a sleeping bag—I really enjoyed exploring. On one occasion we found ourselves walking in a giant circle and ended up laughing hysterically about my lack of direction. As we made our way in a different direction, we stumbled on a fantastic restaurant and had a delicious moonlit dinner. Although very tired, we both appreciated our stamina before taking a taxi back to our hotel. No more walking!

I will say Walter is exhausting. He is on the go from morning to night and I just am not used to moving all day without a break. Then I remembered I am not working and he is working in a very demanding environment so this was probably a slow pace for him. Each night, I was exhausted. Even though I exercise by swimming and walking my dog, Walter was on a 10,000 steps a day program from work and he intended to walk 10,000 steps every day, which meant I too am walking 10,000 steps. Whew!

As I said you really get to know a person when you spend day and night together, and Walter is very adventurous, but so am I. That is on the ground not in the air. So we went to the Capilano Suspension Bridge and I actually made my way across it while clinging to Walter. He had the nail marks to prove it. I was terrified but kept a smile on my face because he was thrilled. Something more my speed was the Butchart Gardens. Although it was raining we loved the color and beauty of all the flowers, trees, and bushes. We finished our trip attending the Arts Club theater production of *Dream Girls*. Fantastic!

The outcome of our Vancouver trip was that we loved being in each other's company and would sometimes talk about our future together. The standing joke was Walter kidding me about being with me "every day." Sometimes out of nowhere he would look at me and say, "Every day," and I would look right back at him and reply, "Every day." It was not oblivious to us that we traveled together very well. As a matter of fact, we talked about it several times making me aware of how serious an issue this was to him.

Perhaps it can be explained by how Walter was feeling. He said he wanted to travel but felt awkward going with a "lady friend." He said, "What if the relationship didn't work out? Then you have to find another person to travel with. How many people can you travel with? How many people can you sleep with?" A bigger issue for Walter is his minister, who does not believe in couples traveling together who are not married, leads a traveling group Walter would like to travel with. Oh my!

Another obstacle is how do you respond to people who automatically assume you are married? What do you say? How do you introduce your partner? Walter and I are not a young couple so I think people automatically assume we were married. We often got, "You are such a good-looking couple, how long have you been married?" What do you say? "Oh this is not my husband?" This sounds so simple but in reality it becomes a real issue particularly if you are religious and find traveling with a person, sharing accommodations, etc., to be a bit inconsistent with your beliefs.

There is the financial aspect also to consider. If the man asked the woman, does that mean he pays for everything or do you agree up front that you each will share all costs? For some men this is very difficult and something quite frankly they are not used to negotiating. No, Walter is the type of man who would not feel comfortable traveling with one woman during a relationship and then traveling with another woman when a new relationship occurs. He and I are both best at traveling with someone we know and someone we can create memories with, hopefully for the rest of our lives.

It just seems appropriate to tell this funny story to emphasize the point. Walter and I were going to meet in Chicago to attend a friend's wedding. He was on a golf outing that he had planned for months but cut it short to be with me. He made the reservations in his name and shared in the notes that I would be arriving before him. So when I arrived I went up to the counter and one of my dearest friends walked up with me, why I don't know but there she was. The clerk said, "We have your room ready Mrs. Oliver." Before I could say thank you, my girlfriend nearly shouted, "She isn't Mrs. Oliver." The clerk and I looked at each other and then at her at the same time with the same expression: Who are you and why are you speaking? I don't know if Walter registered me as his wife or if the clerk just assumed, but whatever the circumstances my girlfriend made it clear that I wasn't Mrs. Oliver.

When something like this happens, you feel a slight twinge of guilt and then you move on. For some couples this is just fine, but as you mature you have a moral code that seems to pop up every now and then to remind you what's right and what's wrong. I certainly am not passing judgment on any couple that feels very comfortable traveling together. I need to confess that I never really thought about the morality of traveling with a man in the past. I had done so on a few occasions without any reservations after my husband died. In fact, as I look back on my traveling experience with other men, I was glad I wasn't married to them. I found traveling with my girlfriends a much more rewarding experience. As a matter of fact, on one occasion I found traveling to Portugal and Spain by myself as one of the most liberating experiences of my life. And then Walter came along.

The Necklace

It's June and I am about to reach a milestone birthday so I decided to do something I always dreamed of but could never afford—take my family on a cruise. I decided to pull money out of my retirement account and celebrate my birthday on the Royal Caribbean's *Allure of the Seas*, An international seven-night Western Caribbean cruise from June 15 through June 22. I took my children and grandchildren, and it was the best thing I have ever done in my life. Walter and I both felt it was too soon for us to travel together with our children and this was a time for me to bond with my family. My daughter and daughter-in-law ordered special red T-shirts that had Happy Birthday GiGi printed on the front with all the family names on the back. GiGi is the name my grandkids call me. We all put on our red GiGi shirts just before we boarded the ship. It was wonderful. There are so many fond memories, but watching the faces on my grown children as we pulled up to the ship was absolutely priceless. It was like watching their faces when they were young opening presents on Christmas morning.

I really splurged and got myself a grand suite knowing that my grandchildren would spend many nights with me. It was perfect. The kids each had their own cabins with their families. When I entered my cabin there was a bouquet of red roses from Walter. The cruise could not be more perfect. So my birthday was wonderful. Even though Walter was not with me, he was in my heart.

The weekend before leaving on the cruise, Walter took me to the Ritz-Carlton for dinner. We love going there because it is elegant and quiet. We have a special table where we sit regularly. Walter had his briefcase with him, which was unusual but I didn't think much about it until he reached into it and pulled out a beautiful midnight blue velvet box. Inside was a necklace with five one-carat diamonds, one on top of the other, encased in a platinum bar setting, beautiful, just beautiful. The necklace of course was unbelievable, however, what brought me to tears is that some time ago I shared with Walter I wanted something special to represent my five grandchildren. And there it was, one diamond for each grandchild. As if the necklace was not enough, he also gave me a key to his condo. He does not like to celebrate birthdays or any holidays with gifts so when I asked him what was the occasion, he replied that it was just because. Everything Walter does has so much meaning because he wraps everything he does in love and because he makes my life a living dream.

I ask God every night what is it that I have done to deserve so much happiness? Why did I meet this man? I am truly mystified. My life has had its ups and downs just like everyone else's. I sin every day! I don't say this with any amount of pride, it is just a fact. As hard as I try before I can get out of my driveway or even speak to another person I find myself committing a sin: passing judgment, exaggerating (in case no one else will tell you this, exaggerating is lying), blaming others, being envious, and oh yes my favorite—getting even. This is just in the first five minutes of my day. Good grief! However, I have finally found an antidote. I believe we are forgiven for our sins, but I need more, so I decided that each time I sin, I will write it down and then find someone or some cause to give something back to. Now you know why I am so busy.

Oh! Another blessing: Walter has a new grandson, a baby boy born in June. Walter also has a birthday in June and I did not even say Happy Birthday to him. Am I a taker and not a giver? How could I not say Happy Birthday to the man I love? What is wrong with me? Even my sister sent him a birthday card and his children sang "Happy Birthday" to him. My excuse was that he does not celebrate birthdays or holidays, but I do! How can I not celebrate the man who is my life? Ugh, I hate myself. Well, perhaps I can be a little less punitive. I did buy him a few gifts while away on the cruise. I will give them to him when we are alone since he is so self-conscious. I also tried to give him gifts for Christmas. They were under the tree and he knew they were for him. I didn't try to force them on him. I just let the gifts stay under the tree and occasionally I would ask him if he was ready to open them. He would just look at me and I knew he wasn't. But one evening we were watching television and he said very pointedly, "I'm ready to open my gifts." I got them and watched Walter trying to act nonchalant but inquisitive at the same time while opening each gift. He enjoyed the gifts and I enjoyed watching him open them.

Everyone loves a gift and I have found that regardless of what Walter says he enjoys surprises. It is difficult to buy anything for him, but I now take a page from my daughter's playbook. She always says it is difficult to buy for me. I remember when she didn't have a lot of money she would write these incredible letters letting me know how appreciative she was for all the tiny and big things I did for her. Just this Christmas she sent me a jar of "Kind Notes." If you are having a bad day or if you just need a word of encouragement you open the jar and take out one of the fifty notes, each folded and placed in its own envelope. Walter and I love opening them because there are also twelve blank notes that my daughter and grandchildren handwrote to me. How wonderful it is to pull a note that says "I love you GiGi for always being there for me." No amount of money can buy such a gift. So why am I telling you this? Because people may not love gifts for special occasions but they do love gifts that demonstrate how thoughtful you are in your selection. Money has nothing to do with it. It is all about how a gift touches your heart. I can't buy anything for Walter that he does not already have, but I can touch his heart.

ANOTHER ARGUMENT?

Joyce asked Walter if she could have her daughter's bridal shower at his place. He graciously agreed and said that he and I would host it. So when I spoke to Joyce I was eager to help plan the shower. It soon became clear during the planning and preparation that I was a "silent" partner with Walter. He and Joyce made all the plans and preparations, ordered the food, and made the final arrangements. The shower took place in the community room of his building. During the shower Walter welcomed everyone and then invited the men to go up to the condo for refreshments while the women stayed for the opening of the gifts. After the shower, Joyce, her daughter, and a few others joined the men. Once again, I tried to assist with the planning in the condo but I soon gave up because it was clear that this was Walter's party. He took care of everything including plates, napkins, and dinnerware. I felt completely left out.

I don't think he knows to this day how upset I was, but he knew something was wrong because I told him we needed to talk in person. He seemed a bit confused but agreed to talk on the weekend when he was back in town. I told him that I knew how tight his schedule was so perhaps putting the conversation aside for now might be more helpful. Time would give us both a chance to reflect on our needs from each other, what we can give and what we cannot give, but also for me personally to take the emotion out and concentrate on why I became so upset.

Walter was still confused but honored my feelings. I could see he was trying to understand so I told him I am always a little melancholy and empty when he leaves. He did say that our relationship is obviously important so he really wanted to work on issues that would help us to grow closer and move toward fulfillment even with all of the emotion and feelings that might be a part of it. He said he believed our relationship is secure enough for us to discuss what our needs are. Even if it is not pretty and extremely difficult, he believed the conversation would be worthwhile and would not destroy our relationship, but build it to an even stronger place. He said the reason he is so confident about the strength of our relationship is because of the Lord's place in it.

Really! That's his response. I don't even know what that means or what I am angry about. Yes, I do, I felt left out and wanted to be a part of the planning and preparation for the shower. I immediately thought Walter must not think I know how to do anything. So, I am angry. I don't know why. What I do know is I can't stay angry with this man.

Walter came in for the weekend to have our deep conversation. But before he arrived I received a beautiful array of white orchids. By the time we sat down to dinner, I was completely defused. Walter leaned in closely looking at me with his complete attention and asked what it was that we needed to discuss. I honestly retraced my planned conversation and within a second, I knew it was not the least bit important. It was my problem, something I conjured up. I was being selfish. I wanted him to know that I did not feel included in the planning of his friend's shower.

Within that same second, I realized that we were dating not married and he lived in the space not me. Naturally he would need to make arrangements with Joyce, not me. I still felt neglected. Oh! That is the operative word, *neglected.* I wanted to be the person he turned to for suggestions. I wanted to be in charge. So there it is, my spoiled selfish attitude. No way was I going to discuss this with a man who has shown me nothing but kindness. So I simply said I wanted to discuss how he felt about our relationship. He said, fine. I said, good. And that was our deep discussion.

There is a song called "Sweet Pea" written and performed by singer and songwriter Amos Lee born Ryan Anthony Massaro. (https://en.wikipedia.org/wiki/Amos_Lee). I just love it. I first heard the term from one of my girlfriends and I picked it up because the words were so endearing to me. The lyrics of the song seem to express how Walter and I feel about each other, "Sweet Pea, apple of my eye, I don't know what and I don't know why, but you're the only reason I keep on coming home." It reminds me when Joyce first shared with me that Walter only comes to Arizona two or three times a year and now he is coming two to three times a month. Wow!

The first verse is an exact reflection of Walter, the last verse speaks to me, "Sweet Pea Keeper of my soul, I know sometimes I'm out of control. You're the only reason I keep on coming home."

We have now been in each other's lives for close to a year and I really don't know what life would be like without Walter. I have someone who genuinely cares about my day. I wrote Walter and addressed him as *Keeper of My Soul* and shared how absolutely safe I felt with him, and in my mind he belongs to me and I belong to him.

The Exotic Dress

As women, we must ask ourselves whom are we dressing for? You already know the answer: We are dressing for other women. I love Chanel handbags. Actually, I love anything with Chanel on it: Chanel #5, Chanel pearls, Chanel shoes, Chanel clothes, but particularly Chanel purses, the classic if you please. I love fashion but get a big kick out of putting expensive and inexpensive items together. Jewelry is my favorite. I can have on expensive clothes but love an armful of costume bangles and faux rings. I also love colors. Every season it seems that I am one season ahead of the color of the year. One year, it was dark brown, another year navy blue. Now, I am thinking orange. Only women are thinking that way. Men of course love to look good in their clothes and often have their favorite designer. Walter's is Brioni and he wears his clothes well.

But once again, whom do we dress for? I can tell you this: Walter loves for me to wear what he calls the exotic dress. It is a one-shoulder, floor-length dress with bold blues, oranges, greens, and yellows. It has a split all the way up to your hip-bone. It is what my generation calls a slutty dress. We bought it at a jazz festival for $69.00 and it is Walter's favorite dress. He just asked me the other day, "Where is the exotic dress?"

When I wear my Chanel dress every woman knows what it is and nods approvingly. I wouldn't dare wear the exotic dress to certain places. On second thought I wouldn't wear the exotic dress anywhere because it is definitely something that would make other women wonder if I had lost my mind. But for Walter, when I put it on, I think he loses his mind. So, we need to ask ourselves, who do we dress for? For me personally I am so happy that Walter still loves to see me in the exotic dress. So as long as I can pull it over these hips, I will wear it whenever he asks and sometimes when he doesn't.

I think most women want to be a little sexy sometimes, and to me, that's what makes life interesting. You're not hurting anyone nor are you trying to be something you are not, you just want to be a little provocative. The exotic dress allows me to give Walter what he wants and I have a few clothes that allow me to feel sexy without appearing vulgar. I have a hand-painted top and pants outfit that I wore on my family cruise that is very sheer but nothing that I couldn't wear in public. I had my picture taken in it and I felt beautiful. I decided to send it to Walter but before I did, I asked my daughter what she thought. She suggested that it might appear to be a little vain. Humph, I sent it anyway. Walter loved it. I wanted him to have a great picture of me to put in his office so he could see me every day and so would any women who happened to be in his office. We women have devious minds and I admit it. I was getting deeper and deeper into my relationship with Walter. He was in Virginia and I was in Arizona. I needed something to keep me on his mind. Voilà, a picture.

A Quick Getaway

Sometimes you just have to get away from it all. Walter will say he wants to take his car on the road to "blow it out," whatever that means. So he arrived in Phoenix on a Thursday evening and we decided to attend a luncheon on Friday and then drive up to Sedona. We really had a late start and realized midway that the art galleries might be closed before we could get a chance to really have a great visit. So we decided to google the area to look for hotels and restaurants that might be fun. Several came up but one in particular caught our attention, the Enchantment Resort. Although we had navigation in our car, the place was an absolute nightmare to find, but once we did we understood why the resort was called *Enchantment*.

We had made overnight reservations while driving and intended to leave the next morning for Sedona, but we found ourselves so taken by the beauty of the resort set in the striking red rocks and mountains known for inspiring the mind, body, and spirit that we booked a spa tranquility his and her package.

After we checked in we decided to walk around before having dinner. We noticed a circular room with a fire pit and a sand floor inspired by the Hopi Native Americans that appeared to be an introduction to the Enchantment Mii Amo, a holistic rejuvenation spa. Arizona is known for its red rocks and mountains. Walter and I looked at each other and commented that once again we had found a beautiful getaway for just the two of us. We walked through the gift shop and purchased a huge disk bowl with horses majestically painted on the outer circle in colors from the desert: browns, blues, greens, and sandstone. The next day we had a wonderful breakfast in the Mii Amo Café and ran into a woman and her daughter who had nothing but praise for the resort.

After breakfast we left for Sedona with memories of a wonderful spiritual experience. When we reached Sedona our first spot was our favorite gallery, Exposures. We immediately looked for the bronze sculpture that captured our hearts on our first visit. There it was majestically sitting in its own private viewing space, and we fell in love with it all over again. This time, Walter signaled to me that we were going to purchase it. Unfortunately, I made it known that I really wanted it, making it difficult for Walter to "negotiate" so I had to leave the area while he talked with the salesperson. He finally purchased it, and while decisions were made concerning the delivery, I found beautiful coasters to give as gifts to my golf committee members.

We had to wait for the coasters to be wrapped and Walter needed to go to the car to get his checkbook. I looked around for a while but wondered what was taking Walter so long. I decided to look for him so I went out the door to the garden area and looked toward the parking lot. There was Walter and two women taking pictures. You might be thinking so what?

Do you remember me sharing with you that every time I tried to take pictures of him in Sedona and other photographic sights, he would say for security reasons he shies away from pictures because one could always be traced by the background of pictures, and in his line of work that would be a breach of security? So that's what!

When Walter turned around I was standing there with a look on my face that prompted him to immediately try to explain why he was between two women posing for a picture. He said he was coming back from the parking lot and one of the women asked if he minded taking a picture with them. Then he said, "What could I say?" I looked at him and said you could have told them the same thing you told me that for security reasons you preferred not to take a picture. Walter looked at me and I looked at him. Then, we decided to not say another word. I was jealous!

When I think about it, perhaps this is why we don't argue: We reflect first and then talk. That's the grown-up way to handle a situation. No accusations, no judgments, just factual information. Well, the facts are that Walter said he didn't take pictures because security could easily look at the surrounding area and determine where you are. If you are with the CIA I guess this is important. Hmmm, is he with the CIA? No! So why was he so comfortable taking pictures with two Asian women? No answer. So you know what happens, the immature mind goes to making up scenarios. Mature minds are confident and simply pass off the picture taking as a kind gesture to tourists. I told you I had a lot of work to do on increasing the joy in my life. I am immature and not kind!

The Engagement

I knew Walter was going to ask me to marry him, and I was certain I knew when he would ask. We had been dating for one year since last October and the perfect time would be this Thanksgiving. Both of our families were coming in for the holiday. So, he would probably do it just before they all came in.

I had already planned what I would wear, a lovely dress, get my hair done, and it would be perfect. This was my plan as I prepared for my organization's Seventh Annual Golf Tournament held in October. Walter flew in on a Thursday and I picked him up from the airport as usual. He said, "Why don't we have a quiet dinner and stop by the condo while I pick up some clothes and then we can go to your house?" I said sure and that is exactly what we did.

After we had dinner we went over to the condo and for some strange reason Walter said why don't you sit on the sofa while I get some things. I really didn't think about it because the view in the condo overlooking the city is beautiful. I saw him come and go a couple of times carrying his briefcase, which was strange. All of a sudden he came around the sofa and sat on the huge square ottoman in front of the sofa facing me and simply said, as he moved down on one knee, "I am not going to mince words. I love you and want to share the rest of my life with you. Will you marry me?" In his hand was the most beautiful engagement ring I had ever seen. It sparkled so that you were mesmerized not only by its size but by the elegant platinum setting.

I am certain my eyes were as big as saucers and my mind was whirling a mile a minute. What, this is not supposed to be how it happens. It's not Thanksgiving, it's the first week in October. What about my dress? My hair is a wreck. Then I heard Walter say with a puzzled expression on his face, "Will you?"

I snapped back to reality in time to be overjoyed with excitement and quickly responded with, "Of course." We were both excited and decided to call our children.

I will only mention this briefly because I knew, but didn't want to accept, that our children were not as happy to hear the news as I would have liked. I called my daughter first who is always positive and she was very happy for us. We called his son next and received the same expression of happiness. Our mistake was calling my son who simply does not dress up his feelings and said, "That's nice."

"Is that all you want to say?" I asked.

"There is nothing more to say," he replied.

We decided not to call anyone else because we were both so happy and did not want to spoil the moment with reactions that on the surface seemed supportive but also seemed unaccepting at the same time.

I think I understand, at least from my children's perspective. I have been married three times, certainly more than my share. In my defense, the first marriage ended in a divorce and the second and third marriage ended due to death caused by scleroderma in my second marriage and cancer in my third marriage. Although my third marriage was an ideal marriage to a man who taught me so much about loving and being the best one could be, it was very brief and left me emotionally drained. The gift from that marriage was two wonderful stepchildren who were grown but in just as much pain as I was. Their father, my husband, and their mother who died several years earlier, were both an only child. They had a distant relative but not anyone who was considered close family so they in essence had absolutely no one they could really count on. Many family friends embraced them and said they would do anything to help, but in the end, only one family friend remained true to them. She and her husband have continued to be close to this day and I am privileged to say, remain my dear friends as well.

I still remember after the funeral his daughter, sitting on a sofa next to me. We were both tearful and just sitting there, not touching or even looking as each other. She blurted out, "Well, I guess you will be leaving soon."

When I looked at her, it was not a statement she was making but a question of concern. I looked at her and said, "I am here as long as you need me." She got in my arms and we just sat silently wondering where do we go from here.

I feel very blessed because my entire family embraced my stepchildren. Sometimes I think even today it was strange for them to become such an intricate part of my family. I admit that I forced the relationship on more than one occasion. However, in my mind that is how I decided to conduct our lives. Their parents were gone and I was here. I promised their father through prayer that I would always be there for his children and I would do the best I could to support them.

The Announcement

That weekend was my organization's Annual Golf Tournament and I proudly wore my beautiful engagement ring. When Walter and I pulled up to the golf resort, we pulled in behind Joyce and her family. I quickly ran up to tell her the news. She was overjoyed. I was encouraged to announce our engagement in a meeting going on during the tournament and of course everyone was elated. Walter wasted no time either telling his friends and coworkers about our engagement. We were very excited and we could feel the love others had for us. Walter wrote in one email, "Love you dearly and now everyone wants to meet you and they are very happy for us. You are a big hit, even though a mystery."

I found myself in a state of exhilaration receiving congratulations from everyone. Friends shaking their heads wondering how, when, and in many cases, why we decided to get married. Perhaps we were supposed to just continue to date and take turns spending long weekends together. We could travel together and simply be a couple. After all, we both experienced wonderful marriages to our spouses so we felt blessed. What else is there? Something that we both felt we needed to address but did not express openly was our children. Although we each had met the other's children separately on several occasions, his children had not met my children. Walter's son and my daughter were in Georgia and my son lives in Arizona. We are getting married . . . it is time to bring our families together.

It's Thanksgiving and we invited all our children to come to my home. I planned an elaborate meal for twenty people including grandchildren: turkey, dressing and gravy, greens, candied yams, filet mignon, corn pudding, and of course sweet potato pie that my daughter makes and a five-tier chocolate cake (from Sam's Club). My daughter-in-law brought her famous Louisiana crawfish casserole. All you could eat and all you could drink: soda, wine, liquor, iced tea, etc. I wanted everything to be perfect because Walter's kids were coming.

My family had come to many family dinners in my home but even they knew that somehow this was different. I even put the Christmas tree up decorated with my special bulbs that I collected over the years as well as ribbon cascading down from the top of the tree. Throughout were blossoms of white Magnolias and Christmas red Amaryllises, on a slow spinning tree stand. It was beautiful. My table decorations were impeccable and the family prayer was everything I could hope for. Everything was perfect. I wanted his children to see who I was beside what they had googled.

I suppose the day went as well as could be expected for the first time that both families came together, but it was oftentimes puzzling. As an example, I had borrowed a high chair and bassinet for Walter's two grandchildren. I put the bassinet in my bedroom away from the noisy side of the house yet I found his son changing the baby on the floor close to the guest bathroom. They never used the bassinet for the baby or the high chair for the toddler. But that is understandable, they were new parents and wanted to make certain they were in range to respond to the children's needs. And like all new parents, they didn't want to make a mess. My grandchildren were excited about children younger than them and wanted to cuddle and hold the little ones.

All of our children were polite and engaged in trivial conversation. As I looked at everyone, I became more and more nervous to the point that I began moving dishes after dinner and taking the desserts from one room to another until I finally dropped a three-tier dessert tray on the floor on my way to the kitchen, I was horrified and as I tried desperately to stop the top tier from falling, all I could hear was the sound of broken glass on my stone tile floors. As I looked up everyone was staring at me except my son who realized I was in shock and immediately came running over to help me. In those few seconds I recalled how many times my son was there for me. When my husband died, it was my son who came to my bedroom, as I was lying down heartbroken, to comfort me and to ask if I needed anything including money. Unbeknownst to me, it was my son who quietly helped his sister, my daughter, as she went through a painful divorce. And although he acted terrible when I first told him about Walter, it was my son who purchased a cognac Coach Sling Pack Men's Bag as a gift for Walter's birthday. Finally, the day was over and everyone left sharing what a wonderful time they had. I was still horrified!

My horrification continues. My sister held another dinner for everyone before Walter's son, daughter-in-law, and two grandsons and my daughter and grandchildren returned to Atlanta. Afterward, Walter and I talked about the evening and we shared our feelings openly and honestly. He mentioned that his children heard one of my family members speak disparagingly about his deceased wife. Oh no! How could this be, my family doesn't even know her name, but Walter said her name was used in an unpleasant way. I cried to Walter that this was impossible, no one in my family would speak ill of his wife, no one. He seemed to understand my anguish and then shared that his son had confided in him that he was scared. He was scared because Walter is all he has outside of his wife and children. Walter and his mother belonged to him. He was afraid to lose his position in Walter's love.

I stared at Walter, but with complete understanding of how his son must be feeling. My daughter seemed fine, but was she having difficulty? My son had made his feelings known—he didn't like Walter. On one occasion when we attended an event, Walter and my son were standing with a group of people. Walter extended his hand and introduced himself when it was clear my son was not going to introduce him after stating, "The only thing I know about you is my kids call you Mr. Walter." No one said a word. My son's disdain was obvious. How different it is now, my son has the greatest respect and admiration for Walter and their relationship now fills my heart with so much more love for both of them.

We have to fix this. Walter was calm and held me close as we both silently contemplated what we could do to ensure our children that we loved them completely and that nothing or no one could ever replace them in our hearts. We forgot the most important solution to all of this: Time. So, we spent time assuring them that nothing was changing except we now have someone in our lives to love just as they have their wives and husbands and children. We now wake up with someone who wants to know about our day—our highs and lows—and someone who wants to share, care, and protect us. Walter talked with his son and I demonstrated to my son how terribly important he is to me. My daughter liked him immediately and I feel a growing relationship with his son and daughter-in-law. All we needed was TIME!

FINGERPRINTED

Walter gave me a key to his condo in June when he surprised me with my beautiful diamond necklace. However, in order to access the condo each resident was provided a key but also a fob to activate the elevator to only their floor. Therefore, unless you had the fob or asked the doorman to use his universal fob to send you to your floor, and that could not happen without the resident's permission, you could not access the condo.

Although Walter gave me the key to the condo, he didn't give me the fob so I could never access the floor on my own. When I asked him for a fob he said he was in the process of getting me one but I should wait a bit because the board was moving over to fingerprinted fobs and the fob would not be available right away. Oh!

Security knew that I was Walter's fiancée, and I would come and go frequently in the building. Security would always key me up and so I never thought about the fob that much until one day I was just talking with the doorman while Walter stopped to get the mail. I nonchalantly asked him about the fingerprinting and he said, "Oh, that's no problem we can get your fingerprint logged into the system in a few seconds. Would you like to do it now?" Hmm, I smiled to myself and said sure. By the time Walter returned with the mail, I had fingerprint access to the floor. The look on Walter's face was priceless as he tried to mask his shock while pretending to be pleased when I said that I now had a fingerprinted fob.

It was clear that I had moved too quickly and he was just not ready for me to have full access to his life. I didn't care. We were engaged and we are getting married. I have full access to his life and he has full access to mine. I love him and he loves me, what else is there? How about sensitivity? We never discussed the fob again and I never used it unless he asked me to go to the condo to do something for him.

GINGER

Don't read this vignette unless you love pets. I frankly was told to eliminate it, but Ginger is a part of my life so here it goes. My heart still feels a tug when I think about Ginger, my sweet little Shih Tzu/Lhasa Apso. Right after my husband died and I had moved to Arizona, I sometimes felt completely alone. I fell in and out of depression even though I had family near or just a plane trip away. Getting up every day and trying to stay active became quite challenging at times, participating in multiple organizations, taking classes, joining a gym, etc. But depression has a way of sneaking up on you and before you know it, stifling you into complacency. I fought it!

Several friends recommended that I get a dog and although I publicly agreed, I thought to myself that is like having a little kid all over again. No thanks! But I would often just visit some of the pet stores and look at the dogs, no cats. I remembered a friend in New Jersey had a beautiful cocker spaniel and I thought that would be a great dog to have if I were serious. But serious I was not.

On one of my visits to a mall I saw a pet store and decided to pop in. I was just looking and as I went from cage to cage looking at the puppies, I saw a chocolate brown cocker spaniel puppy—so cute. The salesperson took him out of the cage so I could play with him. As I was playing with the puppy, the salesperson was walking by and she had a tiny little dog in the palm of her hand. I asked her what kind of dog it was. She replied that it was a mixed female Shih Tzu/Lhasa Apso. What in the world is that? It was so tiny, looked so fragile and then it lifted its little head to peak at me with big brown eyes so full of whatever I was looking for. Before I knew it, I had purchased the dog, a crate, dog food, water and food dishes, blankets, toys, and anything else I thought she might need. And off we went to take Ginger to her new home. I think we stared at each other all night because she kept crying until I finally lifted her out of the crate and wrapped her in a towel and put her in my bed. Big mistake.

I bought Ginger when she was six weeks old from that puppy store, a definite no-no if you ask anyone who deals with pedigree dogs. They call these stores puppy mills, meaning the dogs are mass purchased without any real inspections from accredited agencies. I never had any intention of purchasing a dog from a pet store, I was just looking to see if I really wanted a dog and what kind I might like. Then of course I saw Ginger. How ironic that Walter's deceased wife also had a little Shih Tzu/Lhasa Apso named Higgins. Wow!

The store I purchased her from assured me she was a healthy dog. As a guarantee, I was given six months of free health care that included her shots at a veterinarian of my choice and a three-month supply of a select brand of dog food that Ginger would eat for her first three months. I thought wow, for a pet store this seems pretty reputable to me. Ginger is now seven years old, has never been sick, and has received an excellent checkup yearly when I take her to her veterinarian. Her shots are current and I see about her health as I did with my own children including her teeth. She's my baby.

For seven years I put Ginger in her doggie bed and she would get out in the night and jump on my bed, then look at me as if to say, "How many times are we going to do this? Good night."

Although Walter never said a word about Ginger moving into the condo, I think he was not particularly fond of the idea. He always played with her, petted her, and then brushed off his clothes because Ginger sheds. But what is ironic is that Ginger was not that enthused about moving from her home to a condo.

The first time I took Ginger to the condo she walked around and sniffed everything as I nervously trailed behind her. I took her out on the patio, very spacious, and we both sat out there looking at each other. When you have a pet as long as I had Ginger, you just know what that pet is thinking. And as we sat next to each other on a chaise lounge similar to the one we have at my home, Ginger was thinking, What am I supposed to do out here? I was thinking I could buy one of those portable grass beds with the hidden tray underneath so she could pee on it. Hmmm.

We walked back inside and Ginger turned to me and with her body language seemed to say, "Are you kidding me? Where is my doggie door, where are my friends, Annie the toy terrier who lives next door? The little geckos I play with every morning? My human friends who stop by the back fence and slip me a treat?"

I tried three more times to see if I could make it work. The last time we were at the condo and Ginger had to go. I picked her up, ran to the elevator, pushed the down button, got out of the elevator to the area for dogs on the side of the condo, and then realized there was no grass. Ginger will not pee on dirt. She looked at me as I tried to figure out how to take her for a walk, which meant going back up twelve flights to our unit to get her leash. Thank goodness our maintenance person passed by and offered to loan me a leash someone had left. Ginger and I went for a walk so she could pee and poop. After, we continued to walk and of course everyone who saw her wanted to pet her and tell me how adorable she was. But Ginger and I were having none of that. I was frazzled and she was not responding to all the attention.

Another issue soon became apparent. I was leaving Ginger with the sitter more frequently. I sensed her mood changes and soon watched her become more and more depressed each time I dropped her off. So I arranged for a sitter to come to my home so Ginger would have her same surroundings and her friends. But each time I packed my bag even for a weekend she seemed to become more and more despondent. Ginger and I are best friends and rely on each other for comfort and support. I was not available to her as she had been for me in the past.

What is happening? Perhaps I can find another sitter who can take care of Ginger for longer periods of time or someplace where she can have new friends, like a second home. I shared this with a friend of mine and she told me that her sister-in-law, Doris, loves dogs. Doris doesn't have children and treats her dogs like her children. They love her and she and her husband love them. So, I called Doris to ask if she could keep Ginger for a weekend. That was my way of checking out Doris and her husband, the other dogs, her house, the neighborhood, and anything else that I thought was essential to Ginger's happiness.

Well, I walked into heaven. Doris is charming and Art, her husband, is wonderful. Then, there is Chance, a three-year-old cocker poodle that stands five feet tall on his hind legs. Oh my, Ginger is only two feet tall on her hind legs. Right before my eyes magic occurred. Ginger and Chance hit it off immediately, playing and tugging at each other as though they were long-lost friends. Doris calls Chance Ginger's puppy brother. I left Ginger for the weekend and felt very comfortable. When I picked her up she was a little reluctant but glad to see me. I shared with Doris that this might work. She agreed and encouraged me to bring her back for a longer stay, maybe a week. I agreed, a week it is.

I picked up Ginger on a Sunday and saw how happy she was and for the first time mentally accepted that what I really was doing was planning a new home for Ginger, a home without me. After seeing Ginger with Doris and Art who show so much love for her, I think I can let her go. They have a home similar to mine including a doggie door and a pool. Ginger loves being there. She loves playing with Chance every day. I made up my mind that I would discuss Ginger moving in with Chance, Doris, and Art and they were very comfortable with my decision. I called my daughter who always has a level head about everything and she helped me. She said, "Mom, you have to think about what is good for you and Walter but also what is good for Ginger." That did it. I took her to get groomed and to update her shot records so I could hand over Ginger with her complete up-to-date health record to Doris.

Ginger and I drove up to the house and she jumped up and down because she knew she would see Chance. I was a little melancholy but in good spirits. I went in the house and we all chatted for a while. Then it was time to go. I feel a pang now as I write about what happened next. I looked at Doris and said, "I can't give her up," but Doris assured me I would always be Mommy 1 and she would be Mommy 2. I walked to the door and Ginger looked at me. She knew something was happening and I became very emotional. Doris tried to console me but I was just too overwhelmed. I had Ginger for seven years. I went to my car as Doris and Ginger went back into the house. I put my head on the steering wheel and became violently overcome with emotion. I don't know where it came from. I knew Ginger was in the right place with the right people, but she was mine. I finally controlled myself enough to drive and called my sister crying and sobbing as I shared with her that I just gave Ginger away.

I called Walter but he was not at home so I sent him an email, but he did not respond. The next day he finally emailed and apologized for not being available. He did not realize that giving Ginger up would be so difficult. He always said if I really wanted to keep her it would not be a problem. But I guess in my mind I can only think of one thing to say: There are no great highs without some great lows. Ginger is gone!

AUDREY

Everyone has two or more personalities. Beyoncé is my favorite person because she absolutely portrays Sasha Fierce as her alter ego whom she is not afraid to let out. I on the other hand, like many women, have another personality but not one I would reveal to anyone until Walter. Her name is Audrey, my alter ego. Audrey is daring, sexy, and very outspoken. But as I found out while dating Walter, Audrey loves to come out under the pretense of being funny, creating a joke or a dare if you will.

On one occasion, Walter and I were at his condo and I was changing into more comfortable clothing. I had on black stockings and wanted to take them off. As I sat in the bathroom on the platform tub, I began to take them off by lifting my skirt high enough to reveal my panties, which were also black. While taking off the stockings I saw Walter out of my peripheral vision looking at me. To his defense, there was no door to the area so I just caught a glance and then he was gone.

I am sure he didn't want me to see him staring. When I was finished, we left immediately to meet some friends for dinner and a movie.

The movie theater is located in an outdoor shopping mall and after parking the car, we began to make our way across the mall to reach the escalator that would take us to the second level where two restaurants and the movie theater are. I noticed Walter staring at me and acting kind of off-centered as we walked and talked. Finally, he said, "You know I can't get the image of your panties out of my head."

All of a sudden Audrey was front and center. I looked at him and said, "Really." As I continued walking I opened my purse, turned to Walter, and said as I reached out to him, "Do you mean these panties?" as I placed them in his hand that automatically extended to meet mine.

Walter almost dropped to his knees as he realized he was holding my panties in his hand. He was flabbergasted and just kept laughing while saying, "No she didn't." I don't know what possessed me to take them off in the first place except I was just being devilish and rehearsed in my mind how I was going to slip them in his pocket or something. I remembered one of my best friends sharing how she sent her panties to her significant other in the mail to his office marked personal and classified. We all screamed when she told us. You always see images of women in movies giving their panties to a man or hear of a bunch of college fraternity boys going on a panty raid. This sounds so stupid to me because I am more cerebral except when Audrey comes out. What's that about? Why couldn't I do something like that? Well, I did and now I know why women do it because it works. Every man, if he tells the truth, would love to have a panty experience.

Walter was completely out of it for the rest of the evening. He kept looking at me with that special look that says you are something else. When we were finally alone, we couldn't wait to make love, it was exhilarating. Thank you Audrey. I told Walter that wasn't me, I didn't want him to get the wrong idea, but he just smiled and said Audrey is something else and that she can come out to play anytime.

From that day on when I would pick Walter up from the airport or we would meet after being in our separate homes, it became a game with us. He would say, "On or off?" (Are your panties on or off?) We could be in a public place without anyone knowing what we were talking about. I would make him guess. If he was right, he got to ask for anything he wanted. If not, I got to ask for anything I wanted.

But who cares? Why would I share something so intimate with you? Because you want to know how we fell in love and why we shine internally and externally. We have secrets, a few I will share with you so you can think about the secrets you already share with your significant other or you can craft a new secret to share or you can rekindle the secrets you already have but forgot about. If you think you are too old for secrets or other frivolous things, maybe you are one of the gloomy people who also growl "Why doesn't she act her age," "Her skirt is too short and too tight," "She laughs too loud." But my favorite one is something I heard while I was dancing at a friend's wedding. Someone said, "Close your mouth you look stupid." I was dancing with Walter and I thought I was looking sexy by twisting and turning and making oohs and ahhs with my facial expressions. But guess what, so did he. So gloomy people before you spill out your hateful rhetoric, try to remember when you were young at heart and even though silly, what made you feel so good. I bet it was something stupid, even silly, but you were laughing and feeling so good. Sometimes it takes me a while to understand the importance of the lyrics in a song. But as I am writing these words, I ponder why do we think when we become adults that we can't laugh and be silly? Because it is not appropriate? I discovered the meaning behind "Young at Heart" by songwriter: Carolyn Leigh. I choose to include the entire song here because the words always make me feel good.

YOUNG AT HEART

Fairy tales can come true
It can happen to you if you're young at heart (young at heart)
For it's hard, you will find
To be narrow of mind if you're young at heart (young at heart)

You can go to extremes with impossible schemes
You can laugh when your dreams fall apart at the seams
And life gets more exciting with each passing day
And love is either in your heart or on its way

Don't you know that it's worth
Every treasure on earth to be young at heart (young at heart)
For as rich as you are
It's much better by far to be young at heart (young at heart)

And if you should survive to a hundred and five
Look at all you'll derive out of bein' alive
And here is the best part, you have a head start
If you are among the very young at heart

Moving In

When you move in with someone you just naturally begin to look for places for your things. I was moving from a house that I bought twelve years ago in North Scottsdale, a beautiful four-bedroom ranch with a library, pool, and three-car garage. I loved the house because it sits in a cul-de-sac with reserved land on one side and the back of the house faces the McDowell Mountains. I often sat out on the patio to read or just commune with God. All of my grandchildren visited every summer in that house. Although one of the bedrooms was clearly for them, they immediately took over all of the back bedrooms for their annual GiGi summer camp. They loved the house and wanted to know what was going to happen to "their" home now that I was going to marry Walter. Ginger also grew up in that house, and I did some of my best writing in that house. I also developed some very close girlfriends while there. So naturally, there are memories and tons of keepsakes as well as furniture, paintings, and household items that make a house a home.

Where will all of my things go in Walter's condo? As we looked around, it was obvious that large furniture items were not needed because Walter's condo was now almost completely furnished. What about my art? Several pieces were a must and I soon found space for them. However, when I look back, pieces that were so special to me became items that just didn't go with the decor so I found myself forcing them into bedrooms, bathrooms, or in corners. Two pieces made it into the entrance to the great room but the rest were no longer center stage and had to find a new place to be admired. Some remained in my home and others soon became objects that my daughter and son wanted, so off they went to their new homes.

I am naked without my things and I think Walter sensed that I didn't feel at home but more like a visitor. So, he began to include me more and more into the decision making particularly around major purchases. We also began to shop together for small items like dishes, silverware, towels, kitchen things, etc., providing an opportunity for me to weave colors and patterns together reflecting me in this new place. Just as we completed the selection of furniture together, we began consulting each other on additional major purchases and some minor things for our home. Eventually I became aggressive making a few purchases without talking it over with Walter but always checking to see his reaction. If he liked it, it would stay. If he didn't, I usually would remove it but sometimes I would wait awhile and eventually Walter would end up liking it.

The decorating was almost complete, but in my opinion there were still areas that needed tweaking. For instance, in the living area there was a huge space that made the area look empty. I told Walter it needed something but he loved the openness because he really didn't want to block the extensive window views. I thought this would be a perfect place for a piano. He disagreed, claiming it was too big. Walter is a minimalist.

I want a piano. I had left mine in my house for my granddaughters, and I wanted one because I decided to take piano lessons and really enjoyed having a piano. We went back and forth: No piano. I want a piano. Let's just look at them. We did and Walter bought me a piano. To me, this is one more example of the sensitivity of this man. I was being selfish and he understood that it wasn't the piano I wanted, it was confirmation that this was also my home. Well, to be honest, I really did want the piano.

The condo was becoming OUR home. With the additions we were making I soon felt very comfortable, and when I looked around, as my daughter would say, I saw me in this place. That was important to me. I wanted my children and grandchildren to feel this new space was home.

The Closet

Our wedding was only months away and we were excited as the months turned into weeks. As the day got closer, it seemed there were a million things left to do. I had moved all of the furniture that I thought would work in our new place and most of my clothes. I still had things in my garage and started looking for space in the storage units in the lower level of the condominium.

One day when I came home Walter was in the master closet moving his things out and moving my things in. "What are you doing?" I asked.

"You should have the larger closet for your shoes," he said with a laugh. I protested and said that we could share the space—I didn't want to put him out of the closet. But he insisted. So he moved out, and I moved in.

It's amazing how some things become crystal clear as you observe a very simple gesture like moving clothes from one closet to another. As I watched him, I remember how much he enjoyed walking into his closet and pulling clothes that he would wear. Hmmm, could it be that Walter enjoyed having a master closet? The more I thought about it the more I realized that he probably never had a master closet! His wife had the master and he had the smaller closet. But wait, there is more. It's not just the closet; it is the entire moving in thing. With the unfortunate death of his wife, Walter became a bachelor with a bachelor pad. Walter could decorate the way he wanted, and he could have the kind of furniture he wanted. He could eat when he wanted, do whatever he pleased whenever he pleased without consulting anyone. Then I came along and I now understood his continued use of the phrase, *it's complicated.* Walter was torn between being a single free man without any "complications" and being married again, thereby taking on the wants and needs of another person. I knew he loved me but he also knew when he uttered those three little words, *I love you*, he once again gave up his independence and instead of being an *I*, he became a *We*.

I continued watching him. He turned and smiled at me and I smiled at him. We both knew what he was thinking. Like most couples who are in tune with each other, we have this uncanny way of knowing what the other person is thinking and now even finishing each other's sentences. We are going to get married and we both will give up our independent solo lives but not our independence. We are and must continue to be true to ourselves as we complement each other because that is who we fell in love with.

After his clothes were moved, he looked longingly at the space and then kissed it good-bye. However, in the months ahead as he told his sad story of giving up his closet, he was consoled by every man he talked with because they understood the agony of coming so close to having a master closet only to have it quietly taken by the women they love.

My Bridal Shower

Out of the blue, Joyce called to share with me that Beverly, another lady who belongs to the same organization, wanted to give me a bridal shower. My sister had mentioned it earlier, but I thought I was much too old for a bridal shower and told her that I really didn't want one. However, Joyce and Beverly insisted and asked me to give them the names and addresses of about fifteen to twenty women I wanted to invite. Oh my, a bridal shower, who would want to come? Well as Joyce tells it, at first the hostesses asked me to expand my list because they were not getting the RSVPs they thought they should have two weeks out from the date of the shower. But to everyone's surprise one person after another responded and the guest list grew to fifty women. My daughter flew in from Georgia and my daughter-in-law attended as well.

I was so overwhelmed with the outpouring of love shown to me that I simply broke down and cried. It was something out of a fairy tale, and I was the princess. Valet attendants met you as you pulled up in your car. As the guests entered Beverly's beautiful home they were handed a "Walter and Kay" signature martini. Guests mingled laughing and talking and just having a wonderful time. Then it was time to play games. Oh no, not games! The typical games asking questions about the bride and groom and of course the person who correctly answered the most questions won a prize. Then came the gifts, one after another. So many gifts that we had to number them and color-code them to make certain I would be able to identify the right gift with the right person.

I received everything from the most sophisticated lingerie ensemble to some items with barely enough cloth to cover a small portion of your body. There were lotions and potions as well as panties and bras in every color, fabric, and shape. As each gift was opened you could hear the oohs and ahhs, but little did I know that my comments were recorded. So at the end, a very colorful story was told about someone passing by our bedroom door on our wedding night hearing all of my comments I used when opening the wedding gifts. It was hilarious and so much fun. The only thing I regret is not spending time with each of the guests who attended my shower. As I write these lines, I am falling in love with them all over again.

There were so many gifts from the shower that I could not get them all in my car and told Beverly I would return for them. When I arrived home I was so excited that I called Walter immediately and described in detail everything that took place. His comments still make me smile. He told me that I was going to model each gift for him and he would judge each one based on their excitement level. He said he would send each of the ladies an individual thank-you note for bringing him so much pleasure.

THE FASHION SHOW

Sure enough, when he came home the following weekend I modeled each item for him. I thought he was joking, but he thoroughly enjoyed watching me and I enjoyed watching him watching me. It took several days to show him all the gifts but it was so much fun to laugh, make love, model some more, and make more love.

Gifts continued to come from friends who found out that we were getting married. Some asked if they could take me to lunch because they could not make the shower. On one occasion I received a pair of red satin high heel mules with red ostrich feathers. They were so high that I could hardly walk in them but I modeled them for Walter and they were a big hit. I suggest that every woman get a pair if you want to spice up your love life. To this day I can still pull out an item from the shower that creates a very fun evening.

What is it about women's lingerie that seemingly turns men on? I could say that it isn't the lingerie, it's the woman wearing the lingerie. However, putting sexy underwear on a woman who isn't sexy could be a disaster. I really think that women should be true to themselves. I am not talking about thongs and feathers, I am talking about sexy underwear. Something as simple as a matching lace bra and panty in a color other than white. Black always works but a beautiful blue or green, perhaps purple, and definitely red are real turn-ons according to all the men magazines I have seen. I think sometimes we become complacent, even predictable.

Every woman has the standard essentials in white, black, and nude. And every husband, boyfriend, or significant other does not need to look because he knows you are wearing the essentials. But what if you simply throw in a beautiful red bra and matching panty? Too old for that? Think your body should never be seen? I want to challenge you to try it just once. If you buy them and actually put them on and let him know you have them on I guarantee two things. First, he will be excited all day and think about you all day. Second, you will feel unbelievably confident and sexy, which is even more important than impressing your man.

I know, and my girlfriends will vouch for this, sexy underwear makes you feel good about yourself. Even if no one can see them, you know you look good because you feel good. Remember when we talked about the two of you having secrets? Well, this is also a wonderful secret that the two of you can share. I have a friend that replaced her bra straps with straps that had faux diamonds sewn on them. Every time her blouse slightly slipped off her shoulder you got a very brief peak at a sparkling strap. How sexy is that?

The Wedding

Now, 686 emails later, we are married and still wondering what hit us, what came over two people who are in the winter of their lives to fall so passionately in love. We often acknowledge the love we have for our past spouses I think because we feel guilty and want to be certain that we never dishonor our love for them. This love is different we think because there are no bills, mortgages, or kids to move our lives around. It's just the two of us.

Our love has grown out of a different set of experiences than the experiences we had with our past spouses. This is an uncomplicated love that will not dwell in the past or over plans for the future. I think that is why we were so drawn to and finally purchased Richard Pankratz's beautiful bronze statue called *Waiting for the Bus*. It symbolizes our philosophy in terms of how we want to live our lives, not in the past and not planning for the future but living right now, in the moment, as dramatically and spontaneously as we can.

Two hundred fifty people were invited to our wedding and 284 attended. We were surprised at how taken people were with how our relationship evolved and finally culminated with our wedding at the Phoenix Art Museum. We did not want our special time to be a typical wedding, which is why we held it at the museum. A Joyous Event coordinated our wedding and worked closely with us to plan the perfect wedding. Our guests arrived to musicians placed strategically throughout the museum. There was a cellist, pianist, harpist, and violinist playing to small groups as people toured and mingled in different venues. As the guests moved about, they were enticed with passed hors d'oeuvres and a signature drink. We also had several caricaturists drawing pictures of guests for keepsakes. In addition, every woman received a pair of flip-flops so they could comfortably walk through the museum.

While all of this was happening, the family was in a private prayer service led by my friend who taught Bible Study with me a few years earlier. We wanted a prayer service to share with our families, particularly our children, how much they are loved and although we are getting married, they would continue to be the number one priority in our lives. We also wanted to share that love has no boundaries or restrictions and hopefully we are demonstrating that by loving more you increase the possibilities of being loved more.

In essence, don't be afraid of letting someone else in your circle of love, loosen the reigns on who you let in and you will find that you will receive endless gifts. To me this was particularly important for my stepchildren to hear. I wanted them to know that their place was still the same in my life and always would be. And finally we wanted to have our families pray together to symbolize the importance of two people making a commitment to honor each other but that it could never be complete without their blessings.

After the prayer service the judge who performed our marriage ceremony spoke and asked our sons to come forward to represent our individual families in the signing and witnessing of our marriage certificate. That in itself gave our families, including the little ones, a sense of being a part of something major in our lives. Our sons looked at each other and us with a sense of responsibility as they represented each family. It was very moving and that one small gesture, signing the marriage certificate as witnesses to our marriage, seemed to set aside any misgivings the families had. I am not saying that everything was perfect but in our eyes it was everything we wanted to represent us as a couple.

The guests were called into the great hall of the museum where they were seated at tables adorned by elaborate cascading floral arrangements, silk linens, and formal glasses, plates, and silverware. They were then asked to turn their attention to the balcony as the minister, children, and grandchildren gathered. Next, Walter appeared and finally I appeared. To continue our unconventional wedding, I wore a strapless purple gown with a lilac tulle train that covered my shoulders and cascaded down my back trailing three feet on the ground. I stayed up one night sewing crystals on the train so they would sparkle as I moved about.

The wedding itself was brief but beautiful. At the close, our wedding coordinator took time to explain to our guests what they were observing and why it was so important. The children, grandchildren, my sister and her husband were all introduced and seated at a special family table. As the guests looked on and applauded the introduction of our family members, Walter and I quietly made our way to a back staircase that entered the great hall on the opposite side of the room. As our guests turned they saw us making our way down the staircase as we were introduced. Then, an amazing thing happened. The harmonica player that played "Ribbons in the Sky" by Stevie Wonder under the tunnel on our third date was there at our wedding playing the same song and we danced with as much love as any two people could ever share.

After dinner our dear friend Joyce, the matchmaker, was introduced to our wedding guests. We asked her to give an overview of how she played Cupid in putting Walter and I together. In classical mythology Cupid is the winged god of love who controls the desires of anyone he chooses by piercing him or her with his golden arrow of love. Poor Walter, he had love dust sprinkled on him by my sister and now Cupid Joyce with her golden arrow. Joyce shared how she carefully planned how she would put Walter and I together. She had our guests laughing with delight as she told them how she demanded that Walter and I date, get along, and marry—she had never told us that part before. She shared with them that early in our relationship she reminded Walter and I that she had been working on putting the two of us together for a year and she was not going to let us mess it up by not following her script.

Our guests were in stitches as Joyce shared how difficult it was getting us together. She said it was like herding cats, but she was not daunted by our evasive techniques. She simply stayed on us until we were completely smitten by each other. Whenever I would get off script she would reel me in by saying, "Do you know how many women want to know why I didn't introduce Walter to them? I'm catching havoc on account of you two, so act right." She ended by saying although we were difficult in the beginning she knew we were a match.

She said she could see love all around us. It only took two months before we found ourselves completely in love thanks to Cupid Joyce.

At the close of dinner, Walter took the microphone to thank everyone for coming. He shared how grateful we were that each of them took time from their busy day to celebrate our wedding. Then, Walter did an amazing thing. He talked about how we were both committed to the education of inner city youth and because of this we decided to end our wedding not with the typical dancing but with a special treat. He invited everyone to adjourn to the museum's auditorium. When our guests arrived in the auditorium to take their seats, they saw on stage members of the Inner City Youth Orchestra of Los Angeles accompanied by Charles Dickerson, founder, executive director, and conductor to entertain our guests. The orchestra is made up of students ranging from ages ten to twenty-five, and "The mission of ICYOLA is to cultivate musical expression as a vehicle for personal development, and to bring to fruition the full potential of inner city youth, both musically and academically."

As I took my seat, I felt like we were all in the Kennedy Center in New York about to hear an amazing program. The audience was captivated by the level of professionalism and the complexity of the arrangements played for us. I was thrilled when a young violinist came down from the stage and played "Isn't She Lovely" by Stevie Wonder. The program finale was electric as Mr. Dickerson invited me to the stage and danced with me and then teased Walter until he came on stage to finish the dance. We signaled other couples to join us, and a few did including my Nine-year-old grandson who took my eleven-year-old granddaughter by the waist as she placed her hand in his, and they danced to the audience's delight.

Waiting for the Bus

The close of the evening was just as magical for us. Our guests made their way from the auditorium to the expansive entry hall of the museum for coffee and dessert. When they arrived, each family received a small glass plaque that was engraved with an excerpt from Richard Pankratz's description of *Waiting for the Bus*, the beautiful bronze sculpture we purchased in Sedona. The plaque read:

> *"Waiting for the Bus" is an expression of one of the states of existence for humans. As humans, we are capable of living fully in the present, living and enjoying life. Unfortunately we often don't. Sometimes we live in the past with the excess baggage of past experiences predetermining or limiting our responses to the present.*
>
> *"Waiting for the Bus" [a sculpture] was created to be a reminder to keep life in balance. The past no longer*

> *exists and the future has not yet been created. What we have is the present, new and fresh and ours to experience moment by moment.*
>
> *June 14, 2014*

Walter and I have taken these words quite seriously. Because of our life experiences we see value in not living in the past nor planning our lives around the future but rather living each day as reverently as we can but also as completely as we can, "This is the day that the Lord has made; let us rejoice and be glad in it" (Psalms 118:24 ESV).

As I think about all the writers, poets, artists, politicians, and others who have taken a position on whether you should live for the moment or live each day of your life in planning and preparation for your future, it appears to me that we can do both. I recall teaching graduate students that the hard work and preparation they were engaged in then will have a tremendous impact on how their lives will unfold in the future. I suppose "live for today, for tomorrow we may die" is a contradictory statement to the ideals we live by because everything we do is in fact preparation for tomorrow. We work to secure money so we can provide food, shelter, and clothing not just for a day but also for tomorrow. We are the ants that work all summer to ensure a comfortable winter, not the grasshopper that lives day to day.

However, I love living for the moment! Walter and I realize that we are in the winter of our lives and thus, we cannot afford to dwell in the past or spend time, money, and resources in planning for a future that is not promised on earth. This is why we shared Pankratz's words with our family and friends. *Balance* is the operative word. In our lives, our past is what made us who we are and prepared us for each other. Our future although not promised on earth, will be based on a culmination of our love for each other, the memories we are creating, and their impact on the quality of the remaining life we have together. I think Albert Einstein sums it up best: "Life is a preparation for the future; and the best preparation for the future is to live as if there were none."

> *She had such a sad beginning and he had such a wonderful loving beginning. And now he arrived at a very sad place in his late years. God said I will give them to each other and she will have a good ending and he will have a new beginning.*

The End . . . or Just the Beginning

The Vows

Kay, here and now, I vow to love you unconditionally as God first loved us, and because of the Lord's example of love I choose to love you in that same way. I vow to honor you as God honored us by having Christ give His life for us. And I vow to keep and protect your spirit as God has given the Holy Spirit to preserve us. I give my life to love, to honor, and to protect you for now and forever more.

Walter, when I first met you I had no idea the impact you would have in my life. I knew who you were but I didn't know how your heart would speak to mine. I didn't know that in the winter of our lives that such love was possible and that I would find someone who I wanted to spend every moment of my life with. As you so eloquently told me when I asked how do you know you are in love with me, you said because I have been blessed with love all my life. I see that now, our parents, siblings, departed spouses, children, and now our grandchildren. Most importantly, we have been blessed in knowing the love of God. Because of this love I wish to always be worthy of your love and now with deep admiration and respect, to give you all my love unconditionally and freely for an eternity.

Monologue

He Said, She Said: A Few of the 686 Emails

SHE SAID:

What a wonderful surprise to wake up and find such a lovely email from you. I too enjoyed being with you. You make me feel special and no one has made me feel that way in a long time. We have memories . . . how special. Be safe and come back as soon as you can.

HE SAID:

I had a wonderful time with you and Ginger over the last few days. Thanks for letting me get to know you and myself during our time together. I will make every effort to make some of the dates during the next few months to be with you, but until then I have memories of great times and the basis to dream and pray about what could be in the future. Rest or sleep well and be granted peace.

SHE SAID:

I'm thinking about you. Are you thinking about me?

HE SAID:

YES, I am thinking about you, I can't get you out of my mind. Just got back from a business meeting dinner, and am going to bed thinking about you.

SHE SAID:

I like the way you talk with your hands. I like your eyes. I like the way you put your hands in your pockets while walking around observing everything—nothing goes unnoticed. I like the way you stand close to me and . . . I love dancing with you!

HE SAID:

Thank you for another amazing day. Your total beauty and companionship draw me closer to completeness every time we are together. And as I discover more of you and me afresh I pray we find God's complete Will. I hope you slept well as I look forward to a new day with you.

SHE SAID:

So, you have a great day knowing that you are blessed and therefore nothing will come to you that you can't handle. Love Sneaky. Yes, I signed off as Sneaky, because I am sneaky, after all . . . I snuck into your heart!

HE SAID:

I do know my love for you is growing so I will have to develop an appropriate email close that is not a mystery. In fact, it could have been a keystroke error, I get so excited when I write or think about you I am surprised I didn't hit the delete key by mistake and have to type it over again. May God grant you peace and my love.

SHE SAID:

I wanted you to know that you woke up this morning wrapped up in my love for you. Have a terrific week

HE SAID:

I will now that I know this, can't wait to be with you.

SHE SAID:

Today I received your beautiful roses. Thank you! I feel very sentimental because the thought behind the roses is so beautiful. I am more convinced each day that you really do love me. So, the second stanza is from Natalie Cole's "Tell Me You Love Me." Tell me that your eyes see only me.

HE SAID:

The closer I get to you the warmer and more satisfied I feel. I am starting the trip now to get even closer.

SHE SAID:

I am hoping to talk with you on the weekend but I remembered you have some evening events so a lovely weekend wakeup call would be wonderful. I am having dinner with the girls tomorrow evening, a breakfast fashion show on Saturday morning, and my granddaughter's birthday party on Sunday afternoon after church.

HE SAID:

I will call you this weekend maybe several times but I will keep trying until I get you. I have a dinner every night this weekend starting tonight. But I will keep calling just to hear your voice even if it is your phone message recording. Your Love.

SHE SAID:

I just received four stems of white orchids, at least twenty blooms, in a beautiful deep red wooded bowl. I don't know what to say, there are no words to describe how you have impacted my life. Thank you! Every time I think I have figured you out you respond in the direct opposite. Nothing to do but surrender to love: the highs, the lows, and everything in between. Too late, I will never let you go.

HE SAID:

I sent you orchids for the following purpose: I wanted to share with you a longer lasting representation of two attributes of our relationship than represented by sending the previous flowers. So first, I chose orchids versus roses for a longer lasting memory. And second, I sent two orchids representing two of the many characteristics attributed to orchids. WHOLENESS and LOVE. So as you look at these flowers know that they were sent to reflect the wholeness and love of our relationship. Your Love.

SHE SAID:

Hello my love, I was online when your email came in. We had a wonderful time, as you would say, magical times—fun, serious, devilish, spiritual, and romantic. I know you are busy, don't worry about me, I am in love and I am loved. I am thinking of some new things to make certain that I remain front and center in your thinking;) Love you more.

HE SAID:

As I get to know more of you, the more I love the wholeness of you. Think of you often, and in various dimensions such as looks, words, touches, companionship, love making, spiritual inspiration, challenges, emotions, and hopes for the future. It just is magical love.

SHE SAID:

I thought about you all day after such a profound email yesterday. I don't know what to say, if in fact I am supposed to say anything. Your last line says it all, it just is magical love. Call me tonight after you are settled. What a wonderful thing it is to be in love. I wish you the grace of God to have everything you need to be happy. Thinking of you and missing your touch.

HE SAID:

You give me joy!

SHE SAID:

I prayed for you and think of you now as I am leaving for the gym. God made you who you are so you could be all that you can be to others. I am thankful to God for you, as I know those who you are deliberating with today and in the past know that you are a fair and just man. Love you!

HE SAID:

Just wanted to let you know that I woke up at 2 a.m. your time this morning, which is 4 a.m., my time and I took a long cold shower. How about that?

SHE SAID:

Good Morning W07. Your assignment, if you wish to accept it, is to love me forever. In return, I will use all my powers to make you happier than you have ever been in your life (or pretty close to it). So today I give our relationship to God, I give up all control and trust that it will evolve in ways that we never thought possible.

HE SAID:

Wow! What a wonderful message. Sneaky, yes you have stolen my heart, captured it and it is forever yours. I love you sweetheart.

SHE SAID:

Good Morning W07. On your next visit you will have an opportunity to try new experiences that will certainly test your skills in multiple ways. If you wish, you may have an accompanist to assist you in reaching your ultimate level of achievement. Don't take too long getting here!

HE SAID:

It was great hearing your voice last night and sharing things happening in your life. I want to support you in all that you are and do, because I love you, AND THAT MAKES ME COMPLETE.

SHE SAID:

You make me cry . . . I am so happy with you. That is why I always want to know if you are happy because how you make me feel is indescribable. I ask myself all the time, is this real? I feel like I am in a dream, the perfect love relationship. Please don't stop loving me.

HE SAID:

Never.

SHE SAID:

Your last email was like a kiss from you, one word so deep and profound. I write and talk forever, you respond meaningfully with one word. I love you.

HE SAID:

Pray you are doing well. Just thinking of you as I attack my pillows at about 4:00 or 4:30 a.m. every night in the absence of you being next to me. I look forward to when we are together again, not for sex but simply for closeness and companionship.

SHE SAID:

Once again thank you so much. Now for dinner Thursday and last night. You have made my life a dream. It's not just the gifts but also the attentive way you care for me. I have always told you that I feel so special when I am with you. Now, I must add protected, spoiled, and most of all simply complete. You might like to know that I have received so many compliments on my necklace. Not just my family, they were ecstatic, but complete strangers walking in the airport, at the restaurant, and the hotel clerk who wanted to know if the diamonds are real:) And now let me share with you that this morning was just wonderful. I felt all day like I am floating, thank you.

HE SAID:

Glad you are having a great time on your adventure with your family. Just could not break the good habit of giving you a morning message of love. Love you and may the Lord grant you peace and comfort and wonderful memories of joyous times.

SHE SAID:

Good morning. I was just thinking about a question I always ask about our love and while reading different verses in the book of Psalms I had an epiphany. Why is this love so intense and so different? You said because we have experienced love and know its uniqueness. I know that is true and after reading this morning I want to add that our love is graced by God.

HE SAID:

I read your email and this one was truly inspiring so I am ready for anything now given your insight about our LOVE. I think I will read a few verses before I go to sleep as well.

SHE SAID:

It's 9:00 p.m. here and so it is 12:00 a.m. your time. I hope you are sleeping because I want you to get this when you wake or later in the morning after you start your day. Thank you for the unexpected but greatly appreciated morning call. I was so surprised that you called from your office. It was wonderful the way a simple call can bring so much happiness. I smiled all day. I think what can I do to make you as happy as I am? I don't know but if you let me, I will spend the rest of my life trying. Have a great day. I love you, don't ever doubt it.

HE SAID:

Wow! What a great message and much needed in starting a busy and tough week so far. During these difficult periods it is so comforting to know someone loves and cares about you and is willing to share their life with you.

SHE SAID:

Then out of nowhere, while thinking about you, the title of our book just came to me . . . *Winter's Love*. Do you get it?

We are in the winter of our lives and so in love. What do you think?

HE SAID:

I love you even though I am writing on my company email system that the email police can see but I will tell the world how much I love you, so there. You are the perfect companion just completing me.

SHE SAID:

Hope you have a fantastic day. "I'm thinking about you. Are you thinking about me?"

HE SAID:

You had not crossed my mind but you have surrounded my heart every minute!

SHE SAID:

They arrived and they are beautiful, two pots of white orchids with purple centers, just beautiful. Whatever you told them must have made quite an impression. Thank you from the bottom of my heart. You have always made me feel so special, but I tell you it is impossible for me to love you any more than I do right now.

HE SAID:

I have much to be thankful for, which includes our love.

SHE SAID:

Yes, we do have a lot to be thankful for. As I looked at our children and grandchildren I felt a quiet sense of accomplishment. They are loved and we are loved, what else is there?

HE SAID:

One minute with you is worth everything.

SHE SAID:

Good morning my love. I feel terrible that we have not shared through email these last few weeks. So, I love you. You are a brilliant shining light in my life and I know without you I would experience a darkness that would leave me absolutely void of life, as I know it now. Thank you for being you. Thank you for wanting me.

HE SAID:

Hope you slept well, I had a pretty good night. I just wanted to tell you I am thinking of you, and look forward to being with you.

SHE SAID:

I have never let myself go so completely as I do when I am in your arms. Sometimes I feel so free that I catch myself and then I let go again and try to give my entire body and soul while making love knowing that if this feeling lasts only a few minutes it's worth experiencing. Love you.

HE SAID:

I woke up at 4:30 a.m. and made love to you.

SHE SAID:

I just thought I would send you a note to let you know that I still get excited when I see you. I still feel tightness in my throat when I think about our love. I still am in awe that you love me the way that I love you.

HE SAID:

I am also committed to getting alignment between these words and my actions, which I think is a pursuit of a lifetime. I am truly sorry if this struggle of alignment is sometimes painful or disappointing for you, others, and myself. But I pray you will as you mentioned stay with me during this journey. And if I ever do anything that is not worthy of such a commitment, then you should feel the freedom to go on without me. I love you, God, and my family and am committed to all of you to mature, hopefully at an acceptable pace.

SHE SAID:

You know I will pick you up. You know I love and adore you. You know that I want to spend as much time as possible with you. You know that you are the first thing I think about when I wake up and the last thing I think about before I go to sleep. You know there is nothing I wouldn't do for you and I know there is nothing you wouldn't do for me. You know I love you and I know you love me. If you didn't know . . . now you know!

HE SAID:

I know! I believe! We are!

On the other hand, I will think of any reason to see you where, when, and however I can even if for a moment. One minute with you is worth everything.

SHE SAID:

Last night I went to bed soon after our conversation. I took a nice hot shower and curled up with your pillows. Your scent is still lingering and smells heavenly. I felt so relaxed and comfortable and probably snored until morning. I woke up refreshed and ready to embrace the day. This is the day that the Lord has made and I will rejoice and be glad in it. Love you!

HE SAID:

So, I will just say I miss you, I love you, I need you.

SHE SAID:

You are on the plane traveling and so you won't see this until late tonight. I just want you to know that I am thinking about you, every day, every minute of every day because things that happen to me remind me of our conversations, which are based on love but more than that, they are based on seeking a better understanding of who we are individually as well as who we are as a couple. I want to walk with you. I love you. Please don't change because I fell in love with the man who is low-key and under the radar.

HE SAID:

Wow! Thanks, this is deep so I will read several times to absorb all the meaning. We are together for the balance of time. Love your soon to be husband.

SHE SAID:

You know I am crying, so thoughtful, so beautiful, so you, I love you too.

Appendix

Survey Results for Identifying Ten Qualities Men Find Attractive in Women

The informal survey was given to fifty men. Twenty-eight men of all ages, races, marital status, and religions responded. Many similar responses are listed behind an identified major quality. If more than one person identified a response, the number of times the response was listed is placed in parenthesis. The ten major qualities selected for the book were the qualities identified most.

1. Attractive: Pleasing Appearance/Graceful/Healthy/Fit/Hygiene/Clean (8)
2. Accepting/Inclusive (3)
3. Accountable/Responsible/Reliable/Loyal/Supportive (6)

4. Adventuress (2)
5. Arts/Musically Inclined (3)
6. Classy (3)
7. Cook and Clean (2)
8. Communication (2)
9. Companion (2)
10. Compassionate/Kind/Caring/Empathetic/Loving Spirit/Warm/Magnanimous/Generous/Giving (10)
11. Confident: Determined/Fearless/Independent/Self-Esteem/Self-Motivated (7)
12. Educated/Street Smart (3)
13. Facing Problems Together
14. Family Oriented, Wants Children
15. Friendship (3)
16. Goal Oriented/Vision (5)
17. Integrity: Honest/Sincere/Down to Earth (5)
18. Intelligent
19. Likes Animals
20. Optimistic
21. Organized
22. Outdoors (2)
23. Outgoing (2)
24. Passionate
25. Plays Golf
26. Personal Space
27. Personality: Positive/No Drama/Emotionally Stable (7)
28. Respects Me

29. Same Interests/Similar Values (3)
30. Sense of Humor (4)
31. Sensual/Romantic (6)
32. Spirituality (7)

About the Author

Kay Taylor Oliver is an educator and writer who has served as the executive director for professional development for Detroit Public Schools; associate superintendent for Philadelphia Public Schools, and associate professor in the College of Education at Temple University in Philadelphia. She earned a bachelor's degree from Michigan State University, a master's degree from the University of Detroit, and a doctorate of education from Wayne State University. Kay served as president of the Board of Directors for the George Washington Carver Museum in Phoenix, Arizona, and on the National Advisory Boards for Michigan State University's College of Education and "The Learning Classroom" presented by Mort Crim Communications and Stanford University. Kay is a founding member of the National Staff Development Council's Coaching for Results. She is the author of *Teacher Behavior in the Context of a Continuum of*

Teacher Improvement, Through Their Eyes: A Strategic Response to the National Achievement Gap, and *Princess Aisha and the Cave of Judgment.* Dr. Taylor Oliver has received numerous awards for her work on behalf of children. She is married to Walter Oliver and resides in Phoenix, Arizona.